A Helping Hand
—Comprehensive English for Caregivers—

福祉・介護系学生のための総合英語

Masako Shimizu

NAN'UN-DO

A Helping Hand
—Comprehensive English for Caregivers—

Copyright © 2007
by
Masako Shimizu
All Rights Reserved

No part of this book may be reproduced in any form without written permission from the author and Nan'un-do Co., Ltd.

リスニング・スピーキングの力がつく

A Helping Hand
—Comprehensive English for Caregivers—
福祉・介護系学生のための総合英語

CD 全1枚

収録箇所
各章のCDマークの箇所

まえがき

　本書は，福祉・介護を専門とする学生が，その領域の学習に役立つように，また，英語力全般の強化を目的として作成されたものです。

　社会構造が大きく変化し，少子高齢社会が現実となった現在，福祉領域において介護と医療へのニーズは強くなる一方です。それに伴って，本来，誰でもが，どこででも行っていた高齢者の介護(ケア)も専門職のケアワーカーに委ねられることが一般的になってきました。人間誰しも早晩必ず死ぬ運命にあるのですが，たとえば一人で苦しみ，誰にも看取られることなく息を引き取るといった悲惨な事例は勿論のこと，人間として人間らしい生活を送ることができない高齢者の存在は，大きな社会問題になってきました。高齢者のQOL（生活の質）と「尊厳ある死を迎える」環境が必要とされています。

　けれども，ケアワークの対象は高齢者だけではありません。ケアは，身体的に，精神的に，社会的に不安定な状況に置かれ，自分ひとりでは解決できない不安，心配，苦痛，苦悩を抱えている人（クライアント）の状況・環境を，支援，保護，治療などによってより良くし，解決を目指すことです．ケアは児童・青年・成人・高齢者すべての人々に必要とされている社会サービスです。また，現代のケアは医療と社会福祉のシステムに深く関わっています。その意味でも，ケアワーカーは福祉の中心的な存在と言えます。

　このように考えて，私は，本務校（川崎医療福祉大学）の英語の授業でケアワークを教材としました。本書はその教材をより学びやすい形にアレンジしたものです。英語学習に王道はありません。どの教材でも熱心に学べば英語力は身につくはずです。とは言え，より学習者に身近な話題であり，将来の職種に役立つ内容であれば，より効果的であると思われます。また語学力には，「読む」「書く」「聞く」「話す」という4技能のバランスが求められます。

　本書は12のUnitから成り，各Unitは，内容と語学技能の両面を考慮して以下の項目で構成されています。

Reading: ケアに必要とされる具体的なトピックス
　　例: 移動，食事，排泄，入浴介助，身づくろい，レクリエーション活動，コミュニケーション，児童のサポート，在宅援助

Exercise: 語彙習得・内容理解

Dialogue: ケアワーカーとクライアントの会話

Vocabulary: 語彙力を強化するために、「場面に必要な英語」の紹介

Practice: 実際の場面に必要な器具の名称や語彙

Column: 英語をより楽しむために

　また，Appendixを付し，介護と医療に必要とされる事項・用語(英語・日本語)を掲載しました。

　これらが，学習者の専門領域に役立つばかりでなく，英語そのものへの関心に繋がり，さらに発展できるきっかけになることを願っています。

　最後に，本書の刊行をお勧めいただきました南雲堂編集部 青木泰祐編集部長には，立案から校正に至るまで大変お世話になりました。なお英文につきましてはJim Knudsenさんの協力を得ましたことを心から感謝申し上げます。

清水　雅子

Contents

まえがき / 3

Unit 1   The Four Keys to Successful Caregiving / 6

Unit 2   Using Mobility and Lifting Aids / 10

Unit 3   Helping People with Meals / 14

Unit 4   Helping People Use the Toilet / 18

Unit 5   Helping People with Their Bath / 22

Unit 6   Helping People with Dressing and Grooming / 26

Unit 7   Helping People Change Their Position / 30

Unit 8   Helping with Recreational Activities / 34

Unit 9   Helping People to Communicate / 38

Unit 10 Helping People Suffering from Disease and Illness / 42

Unit 11 Helping Children to Develop / 46

Unit 12 Helping with Domestic Duties in a Client's Home / 50

Appendix / 54

Unit 1 The Four Keys to Successful Caregiving

1. Communication

It is essential that you communicate closely with the people you are taking care of. No matter what you are doing, explain what it is and why you are doing it. Always reassure and encourage your clients in order to put their minds at ease.

2. Observing, recording and reporting

Watch for changes in your clients' conditions. Carefully observe their facial expression, mood, dress, body temperature and weight, eating habits, and level of activity for signs of disease or other problems. Always maintain the highest standards of objectivity and professionalism. Record any changes you observe according to your care agency's directions and report them to your supervisor.

3. Client's privacy and dignity

The people you take care of depend on you for their most private functions—taking a bath, undressing and dressing, and going to the toilet. Whatever you do, take their privacy and dignity into account before anything else. And remember: we are not all the same. Each and every one of us must be respected and treated as an individual.

4. Hygiene

Hygiene is of the utmost importance. When accompanying a client to the toilet or disposing of his/her bodily wastes, always carefully follow the procedure set by your care agency.

Notes

caregiving: 介護, 世話　　client: クライアント, 社会福祉サービスを利用する人
observing: 観察　　sign of disease: 病気の兆候　　objectivity: 客観性
professionalism: 専門技術　　care agency: 介護部門　　supervisor: 指導者, 管理者
dignity = human dignity: 人間の尊厳　人間に生まれながらにして備わっている価値。
hygiene [háidʒi(ː)n]: 衛生

EXERCISES

1. Vocabulary Check

英語に相当する日本語をそれぞれ a ～ j から選びなさい。

1. caregiving (　)
2. observing (　)
3. objectivity (　)
4. professionalism (　)
5. dignity (　)
6. supervisor (　)
7. care agency (　)
8. hygiene (　)
9. waste (　)
10. level of activity (　)

a. 尊厳
b. 活動の程度
c. 専門技術
d. 介護部門
e. 介護
f. 衛生
g. 指導者
h. 観察
i. 排泄物
j. 客観性

2. Comprehension Check

介護を必要とする人々に接するときに忘れてはならない原則があります。以下のうち、正しいものには○、間違っているものには×を(　)に記入しなさい。

(　) 1. 介護するときクライアントに不要な心配を与えるので、何をする時も理由を説明する必要はない。

(　) 2. クライアントを観察する際、専門的で客観的な知識によって判断するべきである。

(　) 3. 観察の記録は、自分で工夫したほうがよい。

(　) 4. 施設ではすべての人は平等であるから、プライバシーを無視して良い。

(　) 5. クライアントの衛生面を介護するときには、施設の基準に従う。

3

Dialogue   Introducing Yourself

Careworker: Hello, Mrs. Tanaka. Welcome to our home. My name is Satoko Ueda. But please, just call me Satoko. I'm going to be taking care of you while you're here.
(Satoko)

Mrs. Tanaka: It's very nice to meet you, Satoko.

Satoko: I'd like to show you to your room now. Would you prefer a wheelchair?

Mrs. Tanaka: Pardon me. I didn't hear what you said. I have a slight hearing problem. Could you please speak a little louder and more slowly?

Satoko: Of course. Would you like a wheelchair?

Mrs. Tanaka: I'd rather walk, if you'll walk slowly with me.

Satoko: No problem. Here, take hold of my arm.

(They walk together to Mrs. Tanaka's room.)

Satoko: Here we are. This is your room. It's a semi-private room, so you'll be sharing it with one other person. Here are your pajamas and slippers. Shall I help you get them on?

Mrs. Tanaka: No, thank you. I think I can manage myself. Thanks for your kindness.

Satoko: It's my pleasure. Mrs. Tanaka, why don't you go ahead and change your clothes and take a short rest? I'll be back later. If you have any questions, feel free to ask me then.

Mrs. Tanaka: Thank you. I am a little tired.

知っておきたい英語 ◆◆◆◆◆◆◆◆◆◆◆◆◆◆◆◆◆◆◆◆◆◆◆◆◆◆◆◆◆◆

care: 世話、保護、介護、ケア、管理。福祉領域では、care をカタカナ語で用いる場合が多い。例: ケアプラン(care plan)、ケアマネジメント(care management)、ケアワーカー(careworker)。care は、身体的、精神的に不安定な状況にあって、不安、心配、苦痛、苦悩を覚えているクライアント(ケアの受け手)と、保護、配慮、治癒によって、それらの改善・解決を目指すケアワーカー(ケアの提供者)とによって成立する。医学では、医療、患者管理の意味。 参考: cure: 治癒, treatment: 治療

careworker: この類語については p.12「知っておきたい英語」を参照。

client: クライアント。ユーザー(user)とも言う。一般的には、依頼人、顧客、患者を意味する。福祉においては、専門的な社会福祉サービスを受ける人、その家族、コミュニティを意味する。

patient: 患者。病気や障害をもち、医師に治療を受けている人。

Practice

以下の部屋のイラストで，次の用語を確認しましょう。

bed, pillow, blanket, television, slippers, trash [garbage] box, tea pot, tea cup, refrigerator, closet [locker, wardrobe], light switch, IV [intravenous]
(下記単語はイラストにありませんが付記。)
thermometer, urinal, blood pressure cuff, wash basin, towel, tissue paper, table, telephone

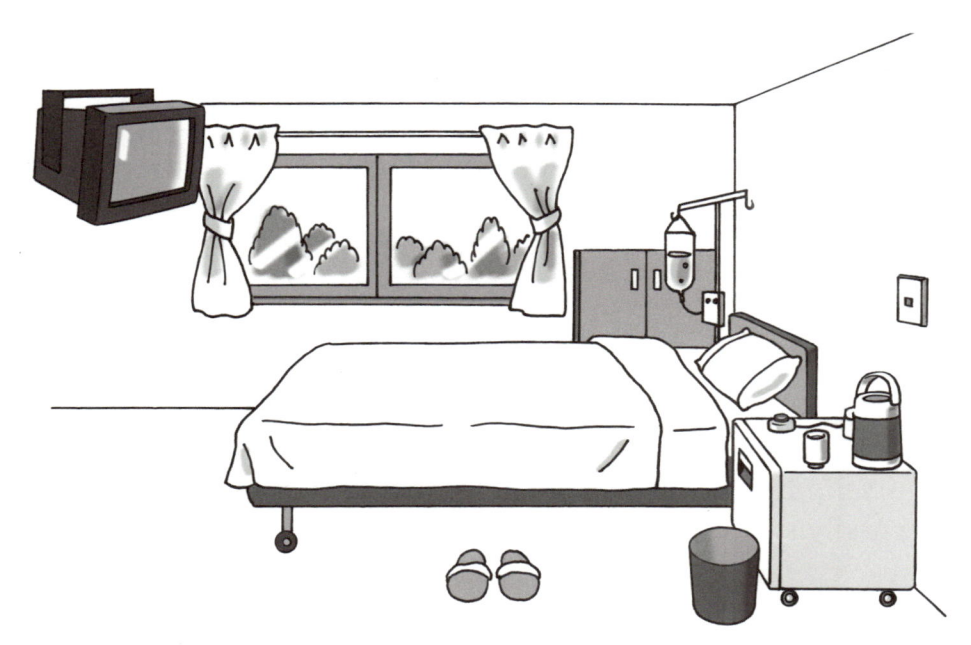

Column

所変われば挨拶 (greeting) 変わる

　人は性格や立場によって日常の振る舞いも異なります。けれども，挨拶は社会生活における基本であることは言うまでもありません。
　施設でも，「元気ですか」("How are you doing?")「気分はどうですか？」("How do you feel today?")「おかげさまで。まあまあです」("Thanks for asking. Not so bad.")などという挨拶がよく交わされるでしょう。挨拶は人々の生活を円滑にする key (てがかり) ともなります。
　ところで，挨拶は世界中おなじというわけではありません。 日本語の決まり文句の「行ってきます。」は，"See you tonight." (夜，帰宅する場合)，"I'll be leaving now."(もう出かけるよ)，あるいは，単に "See you."，"Bye." など。「行ってらっしゃい。」も，"See you." とか，"Bye." というように言い換えます。あるいは，物騒な世の中です。"Take care." (気をつけて) と言ったほうがよいかもしれません。
　それにしても日本語は時として便利です。 仕事が終わった時も，中座する時も，人に問いかける時も，わびる時も「失礼します。」で済むのですから。 これを英語で言うとなると，"I must be going now."，"May I leave now?"，"Excuse me a moment."，"Sorry to interrupt you, but..."，"Excuse me, but 〜"，"I beg your pardon."，"I am sorry 〜"，"Thank you for 〜" というように，状況に応じて表現を変える必要があります。さて，日本語は便利なのでしょうか？

Unit 2: Using Mobility and Lifting Aids

🔊 4

As a careworker, one of your main duties will be to help elderly or disabled people move around using mobility and/or lifting aids. Your home has many different mobility aids, including wheelchairs, walkers, stretchers, and transfer boards, as well as special shoes and artificial arms and legs. Lifting aids include hoists, stair-lifts and slings.

Before using these aids, make sure you receive hands-on instruction from your supervisor in their proper use. Explain exactly what you will be doing to your client. Demonstrating beforehand how an aid works is very effective in gaining your client's trust and putting him/her at ease.

When using aids, keep these two basic priorities in mind. First, although no care worker would ever intentionally hurt a client, accidents do happen, so be especially careful. Second, take care not to hurt yourself. Lifting people and helping them get around is a hard job. You can easily strain your back or pull a muscle.

To prevent accidents, always wear the proper clothing. A loose-fitting shirt, for example, can get caught up in a lifting aid.

Again, remember to talk with and encourage your client at all times. Communication is a vital part of the care-giving process.

Notes

mobility aids: (複数形で)移動補助器具　　lifting aids: 移乗補助器具
disabled person: 障害者　　wheelchair: 車椅子　cf. electric wheelchair 電動車椅子
walker: 歩行器　　stretcher: 担架　　transfer board: トランスファーボード(移乗用板)
artificial arm and leg: 義手と義足　　hoist: ホイスト　　stair-lift: 昇降機　　sling: 吊り具
hands-on instruction: 実際的な説明・指導

EXERCISES

1. Vocabulary Check

英語に相当する日本語をそれぞれ a～j から選びなさい。

1. mobility aids ( )
2. walker ( )
3. artificial leg ( )
4. stretcher ( )
5. stair-lift ( )
6. hands-on instruction ( )
7. muscle ( )
8. sling ( )
9. strain ( )
10. priority ( )

a. 損傷を受ける
b. 優先
c. 実際的な指導
d. 筋肉
e. 吊り具
f. 担架
g. 移動補助器具
h. 歩行器
i. 義足
j. 昇降機

2. Comprehension Check

補助器具を操作するときの注意事項について以下のうち, 正しいものには○, 間違っているものには×を( )に記入しなさい。

( ) 1. 補助器具を操作する前に, クライアントの前で実際に操作をして見せる必要はない。

( ) 2. 補助器具を操作する時, 何よりもクライアントに怪我がないように注意する。

( ) 3. 補助器具操作の際には, ケアワーカーが怪我をする可能性がある。

( ) 4. 事故を防ぐには, ケアワーカーの服装は活動的であればよい。

( ) 5. 補助器具を操作する時は, 安全第一で, 人間的な触れ合いはしなくてよい。

5

Dialogue   In the Garden on a Fine Spring Day

Careworker: Mr. Ashida, would you like to join us for tea in the garden this
(Ms. Hara)   afternoon? It's such a nice day. No wind at all and not a cloud in
               the sky.

Mr. Ashida: Would it be all right if I stayed in my room? I don't feel like going
               outside today.

Ms. Hara: Aren't you feeling well? You look fine.

Mr. Ashida: It's not that. To tell the truth, I don't really enjoy talking with the
               others.

Ms. Hara: Well, you don't necessarily have to talk with anyone. I'm sure
               you'll have a good time just looking at the flowers. Many are just
               coming into bloom.

Mr. Ashida: So early?

Ms. Hara: Yes, and they're lovely. Say, why don't we go out and look at those
               tulips you planted last autumn?

Mr. Ashida: Well, all right. I would like to see how they're doing.

Ms. Hara: That's the spirit. Let me push your wheelchair for you.

(They arrive in the garden.)

Ms. Hara: Oh, look at your tulips. They're beautiful.

Mr. Ashida: They *are* beautiful. You know, I feel better already. Thank you. I
               think I can manage my wheelchair on my own now.

Ms. Hara: Well, if you want tea and cookies, they're on the table over there
               where the others are gathering.

知っておきたい英語

＊介護, 看護, 世話をする人の呼称

careworker: ケアワーカー。(専門的知識・技術をもって, 社会福祉・医療機関や施設, あるいは居宅で, 高齢者や心身に障害があり日常生活を十分かつ適切に行えない人に対して, 身辺の世話や家事を直接援助する。また, 介護の指導や介護提供の計画を行う。介護職員とも言われる。介護福祉士, ケアマネージャーなどの専門資格があるが, 自立支援の単純労働等, 仕事の内容は多様である。イギリスやドイツでは, 医療行為の一部に携わる。)

home help (home helper): 訪問介護員, ホームヘルパー。(介護を必要とする人の家庭を訪れ, 衣食住の世話をする。また, 技術だけではなく, 利用者の病的状態への医療知識を必要とし, 心身のケアにも関わる必要がある。しかし, 現在, ヘルパー資格修得課程(研修終了証)を必要としたり, 雇用条件不良などの問題が起きることもある。)

caregiver: (米) 介護者。通例在宅で老人, 障害者, 病人などを無報酬で世話をする人。(英) carer。

caretaker: (米) 養育者　介護者。世話をする人。例; 教員, 両親, 看護師, 介護士。

care attendant: (英) 重度障害者のために派遣されるホームヘルパー。

care manager: (日本の)介護支援専門員。

Practice　車いすの部分の英語を覚えよう

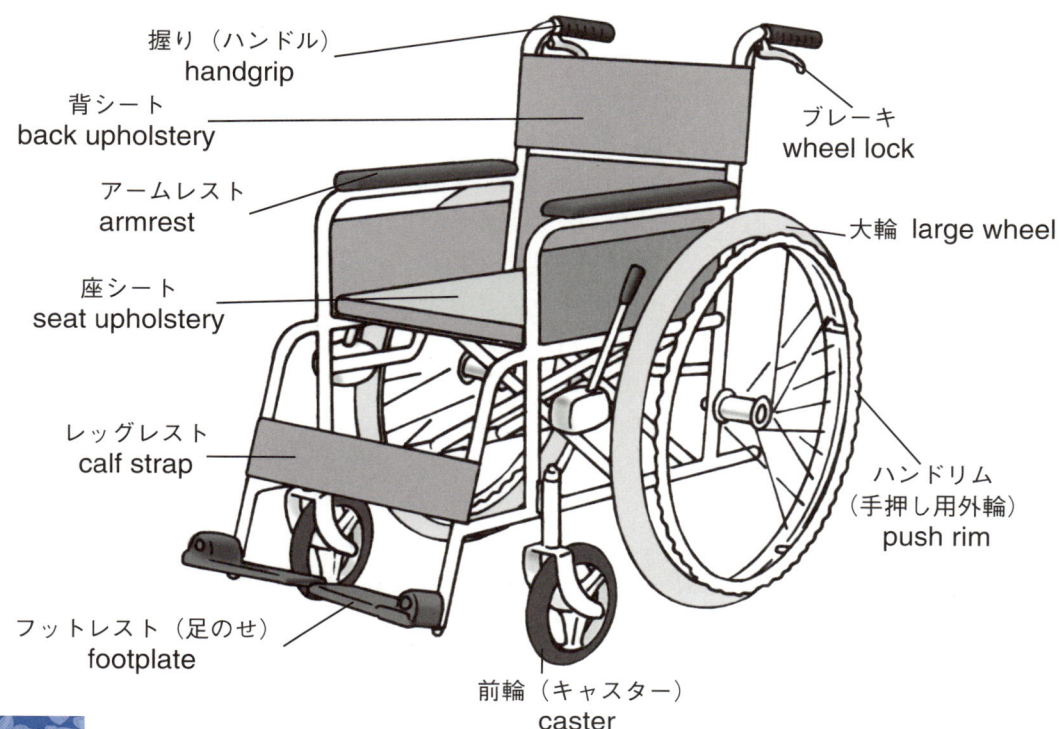

- 握り（ハンドル） handgrip
- 背シート back upholstery
- アームレスト armrest
- 座シート seat upholstery
- レッグレスト calf strap
- フットレスト（足のせ） footplate
- 前輪（キャスター） caster
- ブレーキ wheel lock
- 大輪 large wheel
- ハンドリム（手押し用外輪） push rim

Column

優先座席を英語で言うと？

日本の電車内に優先座席が始めて設置されたのは，1973年の9月15日でした。当時の国鉄山手線，中央線，京浜東北線に「シルバーシート」という名称で老人のためのものでした。silver という英語には(髪などが)銀白色の、という意味以外に silver lining(明るい見通し) silver spoon(相続財産)，silver cord(へその緒,母子のきずな)，silver-tongued(説得力のある)等、よいイメージがあるためでしょうか？時は進んで、いまどきのご高齢者は元気いっぱい、そして、障害ある人に目を向けられるようになり、優先席には，the physically disabled が付記され、最近では次のような表現がされています。日本語と英語の比較をしてみましょう。

例1　優先座席
　　　おゆずりください。この席を必要としているお客さまがいます。
　　　　○お年寄りの方　○身体の不自由な方　○妊婦の方　○幼児をお連れの方等
　　Priority Seats
　　These seats are reserved for passengers with special needs, including the elderly, the physically challenged, expectant mothers, and passengers carrying infants.

例2　優先座席
　　　おゆずりください。
　　　みなさまのやさしい心づかいをお願いします。
　　Courtesy Seat
　　Your kindness is greatly appreciated.

上記の例1にあるように、最近、障害者に challenged person を用いる場合があります。しかし、この表現は「神に与えられた試練に挑戦する人」という意味なので、そのような宗教的概念のない日本で、そのままこの表現を使ってよいかは疑問です。

Unit 2　Using Mobility and Lifting Aids

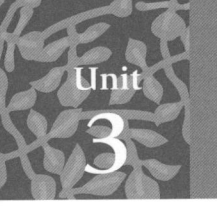

Unit 3 Helping People with Meals

🎧 6

For people in care, eating is especially meaningful. Many have special dietary needs. Most look forward to their mealtimes every day as an enjoyable activity. A good appetite is a sign of good mental and physical health. As a careworker, it is important for you to remember that each client's situation calls for a different style of eating. Before helping your client with his/her meal, you need to make sure in advance that he/she is comfortable. For example, you need to decide where the meal will be served, arrange your client in the best position, check his/her dentures, ensure that the temperature of the food is suitable, and so on.

During the meal, make sure you sit where you can keep an eye on your client. Look for any signs that your client is having trouble eating. It is sometimes necessary to persuade your client to eat what is nutritionally good for him/her. If your client is reluctant to keep eating, try cutting up the food to make eating easier. Encourage your client to eat as much as possible. How far should you go? Your knowledge of the client will tell you how much encouragement is necessary. Eating and drinking are personal matters. So you will need to take the client's feelings and personality into account.

If you need to feed your client, avoid giving him/her too much at once. Don't force your client to eat. If something goes wrong—for example, if your client starts to choke—get help immediately. After the meal, report any problems or differences in your client's eating habits to your supervisor, or write up your observations in the daily record.

Notes

mealtime: 食事の時間　　appetite: 食欲　　dentures : 義歯
temperature: 温度　cf. body temperature 体温, the normal temperature 平熱
keep an eye on: 見守る　　reluctant: 気が進まない　　nutritionally: 栄養的に
cutting up the food: 食べ物を細かく切る　　choke: むせる　　daily record: 日誌

EXERCISES

1. Vocabulary Check

英語に相当する日本語をそれぞれ a～j から選びなさい。

1. dietary need (　)
2. nutritionally (　)
3. appetite (　)
4. dentures (　)
5. choke (　)
6. reluctant (　)
7. mealtime (　)
8. daily record (　)
9. encouragement (　)
10. physical health (　)

a. 食事時間
b. 日誌
c. 励まし
d. 身体の健康
e. 栄養的に
f. 義歯
g. 食欲
h. むせる
i. 食事療法の必要
j. 気が進まない

2. Comprehension Check

食事介助の際の注意事項について以下のうち, 正しいものには○, 間違っているものには×を( )に記入しなさい。

(　) 1. 人は食欲があることが, 精神的にも身体的にも健康である指標となる。

(　) 2. 食事がクライアントにとって快適であるように, 準備する必要がある。

(　) 3. クライアントの自立を促すためには, 食事中傍にいない方がよい。

(　) 4. クライアントが食べたくない時は, 栄養を考えて強いて食べさせる。

(　) 5. 食事は個人的な事柄であるが, 施設ではクライアントの気持を優先しないでよい。

🔘 7

Dialogue Breakfast Time

Careworker: Good morning, Mr. Suzuki. How are you feeling?
(Mrs. Yamada)

Mr. Suzuki: Great, Mrs. Yamada. I had a good night's sleep.

Mrs. Yamada: I'm glad to hear that. I've brought your breakfast.

Mr. Suzuki: Good. I'm really looking forward to breakfast. I have a good appetite this morning.

Mrs. Yamada: I'm glad to hear that. Here, let me set this lapboard on your bed. And I'll raise your head a little. How's that?

Mr. Suzuki: Perfect. Hey, what happened to my soft diet? This isn't what I usually get for breakfast.

Mrs. Yamada: Your stomach's all better now, so the nutritionist changed you to a regular diet.

Mr. Suzuki: Well, it looks delicious. Can I eat by myself?

Mrs. Yamada: Of course. Here, let me tie your bib on for you. And here's a hot towel to wash your hands with. Have you put in your dentures? Now make sure you chew carefully.

(Mr. Suzuki begins to eat and then chokes.)

Mrs. Yamada: Slow down, Mr. Suzuki. Just one bite at a time.

Mr. Suzuki: (Later) I've had enough. But that was delicious.

Mrs. Yamada: You do have a good appetite! Here, give me your dentures and I'll clean them for you.

Mr. Suzuki: Thanks for all your help, Mrs. Yamada.

知っておきたい英語 ❖❖❖❖❖❖❖❖❖❖❖❖❖❖❖❖❖❖❖❖❖❖❖❖❖❖❖

食事に関する英語表現
　＊食事
　　普通食: regular diet　　七分粥: pureed diet with thickened liquid
　　五分粥: soft diet　　流動食: clear liquid diet
　　減塩食: low salt diet　　低脂肪食: low-fat diet
　　　注意: 通常, diet は日常の飲食物, 日常レベルでの体重調整のための低カロリー食などを意味する。
　　　　　医療場面では, 心臓病や糖尿病治療のための規定食を意味する。
　　禁飲食: NPO: nothing by mouth (non per os, nil per os)
　＊栄養の専門家
　　nutritionist: 栄養士
　　administered nutritionist: 管理栄養士
　　clinical nutritionist: 臨床栄養士　cf. 栄養素 nutrients(通例, 複数形)　栄養摂取, 栄養学 nutrition

　＊配膳
　　serve the food, (meal): 食事を配る
　　take the dishes back: (clear the table) = 皿をさげる　cf. "do the dishes" (皿を洗う)
　　set the table: テーブルに食事の用意をする。

Practice

食事に役立つ食卓の英語を覚えよう。

おしぼり
a small moistened towel

エプロン
apron

自助具　self-help devices for eating

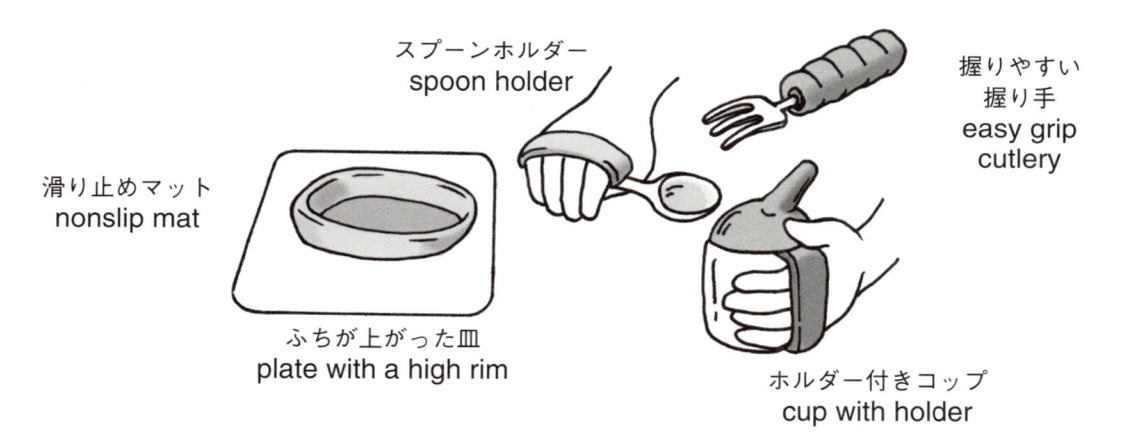

スプーンホルダー
spoon holder

握りやすい握り手
easy grip cutlery

滑り止めマット
nonslip mat

ふちが上がった皿
plate with a high rim

ホルダー付きコップ
cup with holder

Column

breakfast は断食を中断する？

　日本語の「朝食」は，朝という時間帯に食べる食事を意味します。昼食，夕食，夜食も同様です。英語の breakfast は，fast(断食)を break(中断する)という意味です。断食後に始めて食物を口にしたのが朝であったのか，あるいは眠っている間は何も食べないので断食同然だったからでしょうか。英語では，昼でも夜でもご馳走をいただく食事が dinner ですが，この dinner の元の dine は breakfast の意味です。かつて，断食後の食事はご馳走に思えたからでしょう。あるいは，日常は非常に質素な食事だったのでしょうか？ lunch は，軽い食事という意味の nuncheon(noon + schench = drink)から luncheon へ，さらに lunch に変化したものです。supper は「スープや飲み物を一口すする」という sup から出来た語です。

　このように日本語はあっさりと「時間＋食」というのに対して，英語の食事を表す語にはそれぞれ意味のあるのが対照的です。

Unit 4 Helping People Use the Toilet

🔊 8

No area of care is more intimate than helping people to use the toilet. When a client is using the lavatory, you need to let him/her be as independent as possible. Clients may call for help by asking you directly or using an emergency button. When this happens, keep in mind that people's attitudes to their bodies are very different.

When a client asks you for help, the first thing you must decide is what aids you will need. Can the client walk to the lavatory on his/her own? Or should you use a portable toilet or a urinal or a bedpan?

When a client is using the toilet, his/her privacy should be your first consideration. Always keep the door of the lavatory closed. Also, make sure the client is positioned correctly so he/she will be able to sit on the toilet comfortably and safely. In a confined space like a lavatory, it is easy for people to stumble and get hurt. At times, you may have to help a client loosen his/her clothing. You may also need to stand beside your client, or wait just outside the door. When the client is finished, if necessary, help him/her with cleaning, although it is better to encourage the client to do this him/herself.

When helping a client, keep an eye out for bruises, rashes, or other problems. Tell your supervisor about anything you find as soon as you can. And don't forget your own hygiene. Wash your hands thoroughly and check your clothing for stains or spatter.

Notes

intimate: 個人的な　　lavatory: 洗面所, 便所, (水洗)便器.　　be embarrassed: 恥ずかしがる
emergency button: 緊急用呼び出しボタン　　portable toilet (commode): 室内用便器
urinal: 尿器(しびん)　　bedpan: 差込み便器　　confined space: 狭い(閉じこめられた)場所
stumble: つまづく　　bruise: 傷　　rash: 発疹　　stain, spatter: 汚れ

EXERCISES

1. Vocabulary Check

英語に相当する日本語をそれぞれ a 〜 j から選びなさい。

1. bruise （　）
2. attitude （　）
3. stumble （　）
4. urine （　）
5. urinal （　）
6. commode （　）
7. bedpan （　）
8. stain （　）
9. emergency button （　）
10. intimate （　）

a. 差し込み便器
b. 室内用便器
c. 個人的な
d. 汚れ
e. 緊急用呼び出しボタン
f. 態度
g. 傷
h. つまずく
i. 尿
j. 尿器

2. Comprehension Check

排泄介助の際の注意事項について以下のうち，正しいものには○，間違っているものには×を（　）に記入しなさい。

（　）1. 排泄は急を要することが多いので，必ず介助をする方がよい。

（　）2. クライアントが排泄介助を必要とする時は，さまざまな伝え方をする。

（　）3. 排泄介助を依頼された時は，まず歩いてトイレに付き添うのがよい。

（　）4. クライアントが排泄前，便器に座れる位置にいるかを確認する必要がある。

（　）5. 排泄介助の際には，クライアントの傷や発疹，その他の変化には特に注意する必要はない。

9

Dialogue Helping a Client Use the Toilet in His/Her Room

Careworker: Did you call me, Mrs. Ikeda?
(Mrs. Onishi)

Mrs. Ikeda: Yes, I'm sorry, but I think I have to move my bowels. Could you please help me to use the portable toilet?

Mrs. Onishi: Sure. Put your hands around my neck and I'll help you sit up on the bed. There you go. Now, I'll just move you down to the commode. Hold on tight. Okay. Shall I loosen your gown for you?

Mrs. Ikeda: No, thanks. I can do that on my own.

Mrs. Onishi. Excellent. Then I'll wait outside the door. Just call when you've finished.

(A few minutes later.)

Mrs. Onishi: Have you finished, Mrs. Ikeda? Is everything all right?

Mrs. Ikeda: Actually, I'm feeling a little dizzy. And I'm afraid I'm constipated, too. Could you come back in and give me a hand?

Mrs. Onishi: Maybe you need a laxative. I'll ask my supervisor and bring it to you in a little while. Now, let's get you back into bed.

Mrs. Ikeda: Would you mind telling the doctor that I've been feeling a little out of sorts for the past few days?

Mrs. Onishi: Of course. Now put your hands around my neck again.

知っておきたい英語 ❖❖❖❖❖❖❖❖❖❖❖❖❖❖❖❖❖❖❖❖❖❖❖

＊排泄に関する英語
排尿: urination
排便: defecation (格式語), bowel movement (日常語)
尿: urine, pee (口語: おしっこ)
便: feces, excrement, poo (小児語: うんち)
便器: pot, bedpan
尿器: urinal
下痢: diarrhea
尿失禁: incontinence of urine
便秘: constipation
ポータブルトイレ: portable toilet, commode
おむつ: diaper, nappy (英のみ)
紙おむつ: paper diaper(disposable [plastic] diaper)
おむつカバー: diaper cover

Practice

排泄に用いる用具の英語を覚えよう。

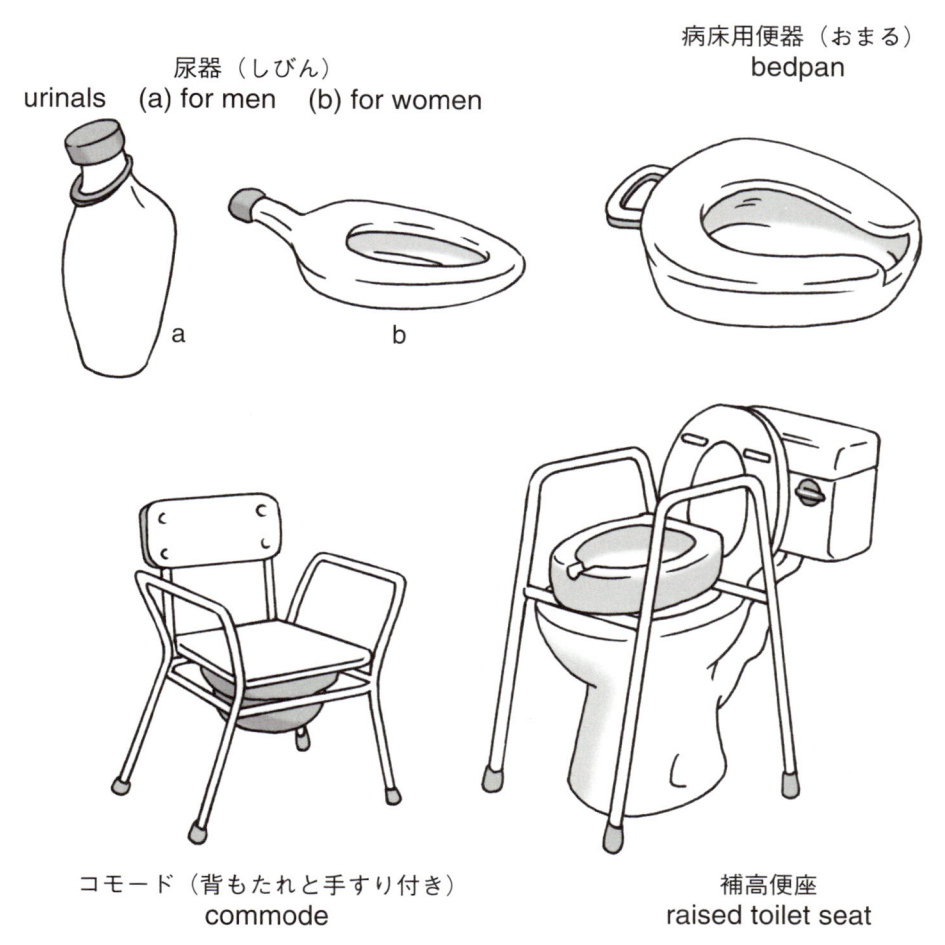

尿器（しびん）
urinals　(a) for men　(b) for women

病床用便器（おまる）
bedpan

a　b

コモード（背もたれと手すり付き）
commode

補高便座
raised toilet seat

Column

トイレの表現: number one は？

排泄の場所はその性質上，直接表現を避ける傾向があります。
toilet(化粧室)や lavatory(英: 学校など)は標準的な表現ですが，その他に，公共施設・ホテルなどでは restroom, washroom, men's(women's) room(米), cloakroom(英), ladies' room(米), (the) Ladies', (the) Gents(英)が使われています。主にアメリカの個人の家では，bathroom が用いられます。このように room で表すことが多いようです。また，口語で loo(英), john(米)という変わった英語もあります。

日本語も負けていません。
便所，手洗所，化粧室，WC，トイレ，パウダールーム，レストルーム，御不浄，憚り，厠，雪隠，お下，手水（ちょうず），etc. 変わった呼び名では古くは，東浄（ちんじょう），用物，尿殿（しどの），一穴，二穴（いっけつ，にけつ）など，漢語や英語の影響も含めてさまざまです。排泄物は wastes と複数形で表します。

さて number one とは人のことでなく，幼児語でおしっこ，number two はうんち，のことです。

Unit 4　Helping People Use the Toilet

Unit 5: Helping People with Their Bath

Nothing makes a client feel better than a nice hot bath. Two things need to be kept in mind when it comes to your clients and bathing. First, you may find that some clients are reluctant to take a bath. Some may be afraid of falling, while others feel it is too much trouble. Don't force a client to take a bath just because it's on your schedule. Instead, try to encourage him/her to take one. Reassure your clients about their safety and explain how important a bath is for their health and well-being. Second, make sure the bathing area is completely safe and properly prepared. For example, the temperature of the water should be between 39 and 40 degrees, and the room temperature between 22 and 26 degrees. If necessary, get everything the bather will need ready, including towels and washcloths, soap and basins, underclothing and nightwear. You may also need to use special bathing equipment, including hoists, trapezes, and chairlifts. Make sure you operate this equipment correctly and with the utmost care.

Whenever possible, the client should be encouraged to wash him/herself. Whether you keep the door shut or not during the bath depends on each client's wishes. Some older people may feel cramped and uncomfortable in small spaces and prefer to keep the door open.

Some clients, like those with artificial limbs or orthotic devices, will require your help. In such cases, make sure their limbs and devices fit properly and comfortably. Also, look for sores caused by chafing and report anything you find to your supervisor.

Notes

The same is true for …: …も同様である　　keep in mind: 銘記する, 忘れないようにする
well-being: 安寧, 健康, 幸福　　the temperature of the water: 湯の温度　　basin: 洗面器
bathing equipment: 入浴用具　　trapeze: トラピーズ(ブランコに似た移動補助器具)
chairlift: チェアリフト(スキーリフトに類似の移動用いす)　　cramped: 狭苦しい　　artificial limb: 義肢
orthotic device: 矯正器具.(関節・四肢の機能回復用の外固定器具で四肢の動き, または補助するもの)
sore: 触れると痛みのある箇所, 炎症箇所　　chafing: すり傷

EXERCISES

1. Vocabulary Check

英語に相当する日本語をそれぞれ a ～ j から選びなさい。

1. temperature ( )
2. bathing equipment ( )
3. basin ( )
4. washcloth ( )
5. sore ( )
6. chafing ( )
7. comfortable ( )
8. orthotic device ( )
9. artificial limb ( )
10. well-being ( )

a. 快適な
b. 安寧
c. 炎症箇所
d. 義肢
e. 矯正器具
f. 擦り傷
g. 温度
h. 入浴用具
i. 洗面器
j. 洗面用タオル

2. Comprehension Check

入浴介助をするときの注意事項について以下のうち, 正しいものには○, 間違っているものには×を ( ) に記入しなさい。

( ) 1. 介護を必要とする人の入浴は危険が伴うので, 必ずケアワーカーがすべて付き添う必要がある。

( ) 2. 入浴はとても個人的なことなので, 脱衣を含めて, 必要に応じて手助けをする。

( ) 3. 入浴に必要な用具はすべて入浴者自身が準備する。

( ) 4. 介護者は湯の温度を入浴者にまかせてよい。

( ) 5. 安全にこころがけ, 入浴中はブザーが鳴らせるようにしておく。

11

Dialogue Helping a Client with a Bath

CareWorker: Mr. Horie, would you like me to help you remove your clothing?
(Mr. Watanabe)

Mr. Horie: Yes, thank you. My arms and shoulders are feeling pretty stiff these days.

Mr. Watanabe: Well, a nice hot bath will do your joints and stiff muscles a world of good. Now, could you raise your left arm a little higher? Excellent. Next, put your hands on my shoulders and raise your right leg. Now, your left leg. Good. Now you can start your bath. Be careful not to slip. Use the handrail when you move around.

Mr. Horie: Thanks for your help. I think I can wash myself. But would you please keep the door open? I don't really like being in small spaces like this.

Mr. Watanabe: I understand. I'll wait outside. Just call me when you've finished, and I'll help you get into the tub.

Mr. Horie: (Later) I'm finished. I'd like to soak in the tub now.

Mr. Watanabe: The water temperature is just right. Now, hold the bar and lift your right foot up and into the tub. Don't worry, I'll support you. There you go. Now your left leg. All right. Don't get in too deep. Keep the water at the level of your heart.

Mr. Horie: Ah! Sheer heaven.

Mr. Watanabe: That feels good, huh. You can stay in there for ten minutes or so. If you start to feel ill or dizzy, just push the buzzer.

Mr. Horie: I'll be fine, I think. Thanks again.

知っておきたい英語

入浴, シャワーを浴びる場面で使う表現
＊器具, その他
脱衣場: a changing room, a dressing room
浴用タオル: (米) washcloth (英) facecloth
温度計: thermometer(アクセントに注意)
水温計: thermometer of the water　　体温計: (clinical) thermometer

＊動作の表現
…を～で洗う: wash ... with ~ : wash one's hair with shampoo
…を洗い流す: rinse off with water
水を出す: turn the water on　　水を止める: turn the water off
湯を沸かす: boil water
浴槽に入る: step into the bath(tub)
浴槽から出る: step out of the bath(tub)
湯につかる: soak in the bath
体を拭く: dry oneself off

Practice

入浴に使う英語を覚えよう。

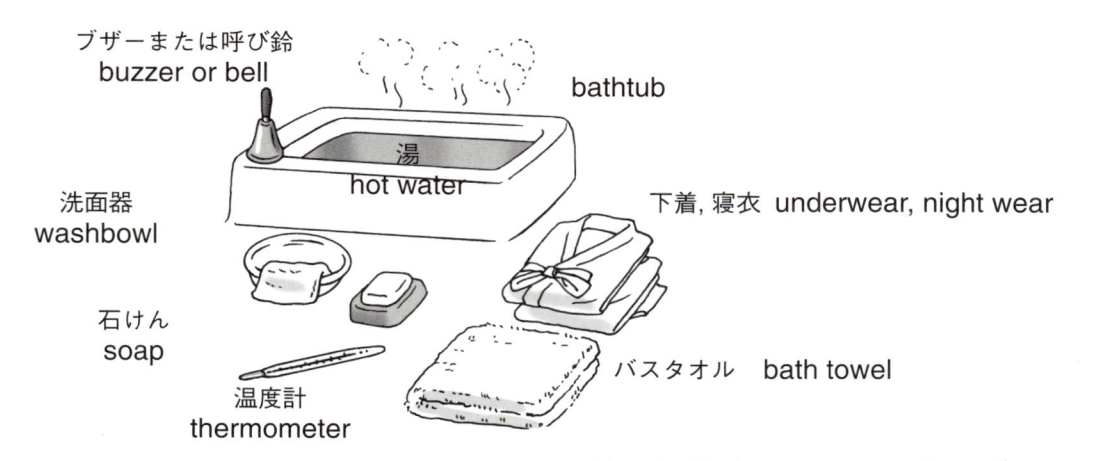

- ブザーまたは呼び鈴 buzzer or bell
- bathtub
- hot water
- 洗面器 washbowl
- 石けん soap
- 温度計 thermometer
- 下着, 寝衣 underwear, night wear
- バスタオル bath towel
- 滑り止め用ゴムマット nonslip rubber mat
- ブザー buzzer
- 手すり handrail / safety rail
- 縁 ledge
- 石けん (a cake of) soap
- 石けん入れ soap dish
- シャワーいす bath (shower) chair
- すのこ duckboards

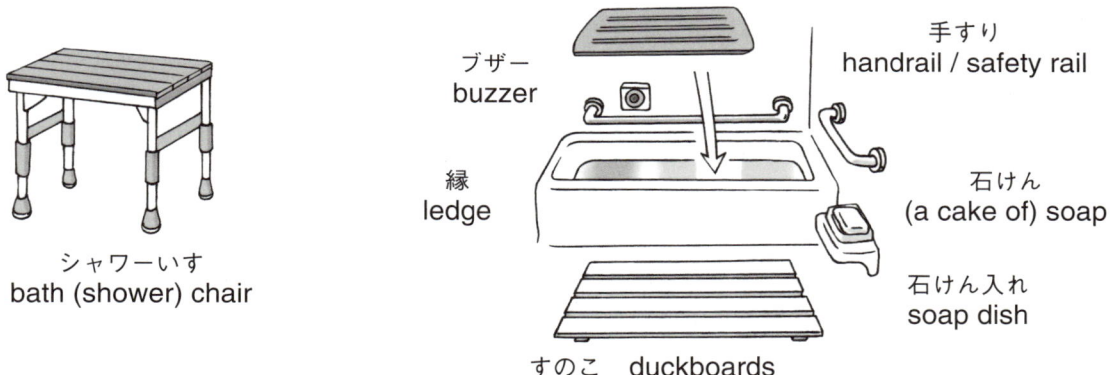

Column

セ氏温度計とカ氏温度計

温度計には, セ氏温度計 (Celsius thermometer) とカ氏温度計 (Fahrenheit thermometer) があります。セ氏とカ氏は, それぞれスエーデンの天文学者, アンドレ・セルシウス (Anders Celsius:1701-44) とドイツの物理学者, ガブリエル D.ファーレンハイト (Gabriel D Fahrenheit:1686-1736) に因む呼び方です。C は centigrade とも読みます。例えば, 20°C を twenty degrees centigrade のように。

英米では主としてカ氏で計測します。カ氏の氷点は 32° F, 沸点は 212° F です。微熱があるなー, と計ってみると 98 度!「え・・・!」と驚くことはありません。セ氏では 37 度ほどですから。換算法は,
セ氏温度 $= \frac{5}{9} \times ($ カ氏温度 $- 32°)$。

とはいうものの, 換算するのはなかなか面倒です。右の表を参考に。

他にも, 重さ・長さ・容積の英語では, 1pound=0.45kilogram, 1mile=1.609kilometer, 1gallon=3.785liters。容易に世界共通にはならないようです。数量計測も文化でしょうか?

°F	°C
212° F	100°C
90°	32°
75°	24°
50°	10°
32°	0°
0°	-18°

Unit 5 Helping People with Their Bath

Unit 6: Helping People with Dressing and Grooming

🔊 12

Most of us are happiest and most satisfied when we look good: when our clothes are neat and clean, our hair is washed and combed, our nails well trimmed. Helping the people you care for with their clothing and grooming can go a long way toward making them feel
5 better, both physically and mentally.

For the elderly and disabled, loose and hygroscopic clothing that is easy to put on and take off is the most desirable. Remember that clothing doesn't just protect our privacy; it protects the body from external contamination of all kinds. Wearing the proper footwear is
10 also very important. When choosing a client's clothing, his/her likes and dislikes must be taken into account. Each client has different needs as well, and should be looked at and treated individually.

Changing a disabled person's pajamas presents special problems, but there are several keys to doing it properly. When helping a hemiplegic
15 person, for example, stand on the non-plegic side and start dressing him/her there. Helping the disabled takes quite a lot of strength and patience, so make sure you are physically and mentally prepared for the task. Also, protect your client's privacy at all times. Never expose a client too long or unnecessarily. When the client is dressed, make
20 sure his/her pajamas are properly smoothed out before he/she lies down in bed. Like smooth sheets and bedding, this will help prevent dangerous pressure sores.

When helping a client with grooming, do it in the safest possible way. This is also a good time to communicate in a friendly manner
25 with your clients.

Notes

grooming: 皮膚, 髪などの手入れ　　go a long way towards: …に大いに役立つ
physically: 身体的に　　mentally: 精神的に 名詞 mind　　hygroscopic: 吸湿性に富む
contamination: 汚染物質　　likes and dislikes: 好き嫌い
hemiplegic: 片麻痺　cf. plegia=paralysis　　expose: 人目にさらす
pressure sore: 褥瘡 (じょくそう)

EXERCISES

1. Vocabulary Check

英語に相当する日本語をそれぞれ a ～ j から選びなさい。

1. hemiplegic (　)
2. hygroscopic (　)
3. pressure sore (　)
4. contamination (　)
5. physically (　)
6. patience (　)
7. mentally (　)
8. grooming (　)
9. trim (　)
10. taste (　)

a. 切り揃える
b. 身体的に
c. 皮膚, 髪などの手入れ
d. 好み
e. 精神的に
f. 片麻痺
g. 褥瘡
h. 汚染物質
i. 吸湿性のある
j. 忍耐

2. Comprehension Check

クライアントの着(脱)衣・身づくろいについて以下のうち, 正しいものには○, 間違っているものには×を ( ) に記入しなさい。

(　) 1. 身なりを整えることはクライアントの心身を快適にする。

(　) 2. 衣服は外界の汚染からクライアントの身体を守る。

(　) 3. 高齢者や障害者には, ゆったりとした吸湿性のよい衣服が望ましく, 着る人の好みは関係ない。

(　) 4. クライアントがベッドで休む前に, 寝具のしわを伸ばす必要がある。

(　) 5. クライアントの身づくろいを手伝う時、安全が第一なので会話する必要はない。

13

Dialogue Two Careworkers Give a Dry Bath to a Hemiplegic Client

Careworker: According to the schedule, it's time for your dry bath, Mr. Ito. May
(Mrs. Kudo) we come in?
Mr. Ito: Please do. I've been waiting for you.
Mrs. Kudo: Mrs. Yasuda and I are going to wash you with some warm towels. First, we'll cover you with this blanket and take your pajamas off underneath. If anything bothers you, just let me know.
Ms. Yasuda: I'm going to unbutton your pajama top and pull off your right sleeve first. There we go. Now, I'm going to roll you over towards me so I can take off the other sleeve. Good. Now, Mrs. Kudo will pull down your pajama bottoms. Can you lift your knee a little?
Mr. Ito: Is that enough?
Ms. Yasuda: Perfect. Are you feeling cold at all?
Mr. Ito: No, I'm fine. A little embarrassed, though.
Mrs. Kudo: Well, don't be, Mr. Ito. There's nothing to be embarrassed about. Now we're going to wipe you down, then dry you off. We'll start at the top and work down.

(After the bath.)

Mrs. Kudo: Now it's time to get you into some nice, clean pajamas. Here, let me smooth out your clothing and sheets. We don't want you getting any pressure sores, now, do we? Okay, we're all finished. Feeling nice and clean and refreshed?
Mr. Ito: I sure am. Thanks so much.

知っておきたい英語

* 病床の英語
  plegic: 麻痺の　名詞形［医］: plegia cf. paralysis
  hemiplegic: 片麻痺の　cf. hemi-: 半分の意味
  pressure sore: 褥瘡, とこずれ(褥瘡の出来やすい場所については次の unit を参考に)

* 着(脱)衣に関する表現
  pajamas: パジャマ. 複数形で使う。a pair of pajamas は正しいが, a pajama は不可。
    参考: a pair of shoes. 靴片方を a shoe と言うことは出来る。
  nightclothes(複数扱い), nightwear: ねまき, パジャマ
  put on: 身に付ける　　I put on my T-shirt. と言うが, 代名詞の場合は, I put it on. と言う。
  take off: 脱ぐ, 外す
  dress: 装う
  wear: 着ている

Practice

口腔の清潔に用いる用具の英語を覚えよう

- 義歯を入れる容器 a container for dentures
- タオル towel
- ガーグルベース(膿盆) kidney basin
- ガーゼ gauze
- 綿棒 cotton bud
- 歯ブラシ toothbrush
- 歯みがき剤 toothpaste
- 口腔洗浄剤 oral cleaner
- 水入りコップ a glass filled with water
- 吸いのみ feeding cup
- おしぼり hand towel

ひげそりに用いる用具を覚えよう

- かみそり razor
- シェイビング・クリーム shaving cream
- 電気かみそり electric shaver
- 乳液等保湿剤 milky lotion (humectant)
- 洗面器 wash basin
- 蒸しタオル hot towel
- 水温計 thermometer
- せっけん soap
- バスタオル bath towel

Column

身支度をする表現はさまざま

英語では、Tシャツも、靴下も、下着も、靴も、メガネも、身につける時はすべて put on を使います。逆は take off です。他に、「はく」「脱ぐ」は draw on(off)、pull on(off)、slip on(off) を、メガネや帽子を「取る」は remove を使うことも出来ます。「帯をしめる、ネクタイを結ぶ」は tie up, fasten、「ほうたいをまく」は dress, bandage 言います。「ほどく」はそれぞれの単語に un を付加するだけです。

それにしても、日本語は、「かぶる、着る、はく、はめる、する、かける、つける、脱ぐ、はずす、とる」等、着衣(put on)と脱衣(take off)の表現が多彩であるのは興味深いことです。この動作に対する言葉の違いは、どうも清潔な場所と不潔と思われる場所とを峻別する必要があったところから来ているのだ、という言語学者もいます。

Unit 6 Helping People with Dressing and Grooming

Unit 7: Helping People Change Their Position

🔊 14

Moving around in bed is often the only form of exercise bedridden clients get. Changing positions makes them feel more comfortable and helps relieve pain and discomfort. People confined to bed for long periods of time are sometimes unwilling or unable to move themselves. Lying in the same position, with constant pressure on one area of the body, can lead to pressure sores. The only way to prevent or heal a pressure sore is to change the client's position frequently, every two hours at least.

When helping a patient move or change positions, two important considerations must be kept in mind. The first is safety. The second is the client's pride.

Changing a patient's position should always be done with two careworkers. Before moving a client, get his/her approval. Encourage your clients to move as much as possible on their own. When a client won't or can't move, there are other techniques for making him/her more comfortable, such as using pillows and cushions. However, a specially formed bed, with a firm but not hard mattress, is far preferable. Beds that are too soft, by the way, can lead to pressure sores and back pain.

Finally, always put yourself in your clients' shoes. How would you feel if you could not move on your own? How would you like to be treated?

Notes

bedridden：寝たきりの　　discomfort：不快　　confined to bed：病床についている
every two hours：２時間おきに　　consideration：配慮　　approval：承認
put oneself in a person's shoes：…の立場になって考える

EXERCISES

1. Vocabulary Check

英語に相当する日本語をそれぞれ a～j から選びなさい。

1. preferable ( )
2. discomfort ( )
3. consideration ( )
4. firm ( )
5. approval ( )
6. changing position ( )
7. pillow ( )
8. bedridden ( )
9. patient ( )
10. pain ( )

a. 寝たきりの
b. 患者
c. しっかりした
d. 望ましい
e. 不快
f. 承認
g. 配慮
h. 痛み
i. 体位変換
j. 枕

2. Comprehension Check

体位交換の際の注意事項について以下のうち、正しいものには○、間違っているものには×を( )に記入しなさい。

( ) 1. 移動や体位変換は、クライアントから痛みや不快感を取り除く。

( ) 2. 体位変換を行う時クライアントの自尊心を無視してよい。

( ) 3. 体位変換は、クライアントの同意を得られれば一人で行ってよい。

( ) 4. 褥瘡を防ぐために、クライアント自身に動くよう励ます。

( ) 5. やわらかいマットレスは褥瘡を防ぐのに効果的である。

15
Dialogue   Changing a Bedridden Client's Position

Mr. Ohno: I woke up this morning with a terrible pain on my back, up by my right shoulder. I can't describe how much it hurts. It feels like someone is stabbing me with a needle over and over again.

Careworker: (Mr. Matsui) Let me take a look. I'm going to roll you over to your left a little. Oh, there's the problem. That pressure sore on your shoulder has spread.

Mr. Ohno: How could that happen? You've been changing my position regularly.

Mr. Matsui: And you've also been doing your best to move around, I know. But as the doctor explained, a pressure sore can spread very easily, almost overnight.

Mr. Ohno: It hurts so bad I don't feel like moving or turning at all anymore.

Mr. Matsui: I know how you feel, Mr. Ohno, but don't give up. I'm going to go tell my supervisor about this and see what can be done to make you more comfortable. I'll be right back.

(A few minutes later.)

Mr. Matsui: The supervisor said the doctor will be around to see you later this afternoon. In the meantime, take this pain reliever and I'll apply some ointment to your sore.

Mr. Ohno: Thanks for your help. I really don't like to complain. I know you're all doing everything you can to help me.

Mr. Matsui: Well, we'll just make sure you change your position every two hours. That's the only way to make those sores of yours go away.

知っておきたい英語

surgery: 外科手術（＝ surgical operation), 外科.

＊間隔を表す英語表現
every（〜ごとに）
〜時間ごとに
every 〜 hours　　at 〜 hours intervals　　intervals of 〜 hours
　例文: The medicine has to be taken every three hours.
　　　　（3時間毎に薬を服用しなければなりません。）
〜のうち
　例文: One pupil in six has the flu.
　　　　（6人に1人がインフルエンザに罹っています。）

Practice

褥瘡ができやすい部位の英語を覚えよう

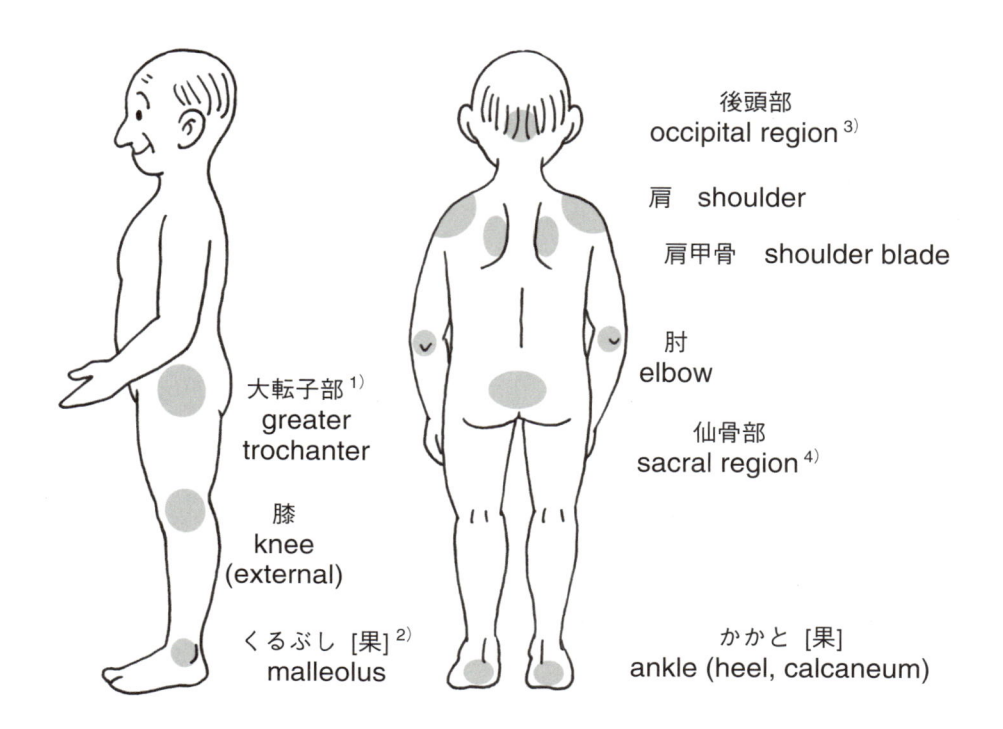

後頭部 occipital region [3]

肩 shoulder

肩甲骨 shoulder blade

大転子部 [1] greater trochanter

肘 elbow

仙骨部 sacral region [4]

膝 knee (external)

くるぶし [果] [2] malleolus

かかと [果] ankle (heel, calcaneum)

1) 大腿骨に近い独立骨格から発達した骨の隆起
2) 果関節の両側にある丸い骨の突起
3) occipital (-bone) = 後頭骨
4) sacrum = 仙骨

圧迫は自らの体重がかかることによって起こり，骨の突出部が褥瘡の好発部位となる。また，外部の物体との間の皮膚にも圧迫がかかりやすい。人が臥床した場合，頭部には7％，胸部には33％，臀部には44％，脚部には16％の割合で荷重がかかり，全体の2分の1近くが臀部にかかっていることになる。

Column

「腰が痛い」を英語で言うと？

「腰が痛い」を英語で言おうとすると、はて、コシはどこを指しているのかな？と考えなければなりません。日本語のコシは曖昧な言葉で、からだの下半身うしろ一帯を指します。これは英語で backside (臀を除く)，waist, hips に相当する部分ですから、腰のどこかを特定する必要があるのです。

コシばかりでなく、「ひざ」は日本語では脚の付け根から膝小僧の部分までを指すことが多く、英語の knee は、脚の大腿部と下腿部の間の関節前部を指します。例えば、drop down on one knee は片膝をついて恭しくお辞儀をする作法です。

子どもがよく訴える "I have a stomachache." (おなかが痛い) は、お臍を中心とした部分の痛みであることが多く、stomach は厳密には「胃」を指しますが、一般には「腹」の意味で用います。「腹」は英語では発話のレベルに合わせて、belly, tummy(幼児・直接表現をさける女性語)，gut(男性・下品な語)，abdomen(腹部の解剖学用語) 等々、使い分けられています。

このように身体用語にターゲットをあてて英語を学ぶのも一興です。

Unit 8: Helping with Recreational Activities

🎧 16

The word "recreation" literally means "to create again." Recreation refers to any daily life activity that makes us more cheerful and comfortable and increases our pleasure. In the field of caregiving, the word recreation means something well beyond activities such as sports and games, singing and dancing, drawing and painting. It includes any activity that helps the people you care for to be more active and alert, both physically and mentally. You'll find that practically any form of recreation can help your clients recover their energy, sense of joy, and will to live.

All care institutions include various recreational activities in their daily schedules. But remember: the kinds of activities a person prefers and his/her physical and mental condition should always be taken into account. Some clients are simply not interested in or up to certain activities. Never force a client to join in. Give the client time to find what he/she likes. It is also, of course, your responsibility to keep an eye on clients during an activity to make sure no one gets hurt.

After the activity is completed, note in your daily record the kind of activity it was, how much time was spent on it, and how successful it was. Ask your clients about their reaction to the activity. Did they enjoy or not enjoy it? Was it too strenuous or too easy? Get them to tell you their true feelings. Also, encourage them to talk about the activity with each other.

Notes

recreation: レクリエーション, 休養, 娯楽, 気晴らし　　literally: 文字どおりに
daily life activity: 日常生活動作 (= ADL; p.52 参照)　　alert: 機敏な　　care institution: 介護施設
take into account: 考慮する　　are not up to: 〜に出来ない　　responsibility: 責任
strenuous: 激しい

EXERCISES

1. Vocabulary Check

英語に相当する日本語をそれぞれ a 〜 j から選びなさい。

1. care institution (　)　　a. 満足感
2. daily schedule (　)　　b. 責任
3. pleasure (　)　　c. 活動
4. strenuous (　)　　d. 反応
5. alert (　)　　e. 日課表
6. activity (　)　　f. 介護施設
7. responsibility (　)　　g. 喜び
8. reaction (　)　　h. 愉快な
9. sense of joy (　)　　i. 激しい
10. cheerful (　)　　j. 機敏な

2. Comprehension Check

クライアントの身づくろいについて，以下のうち正しいものには○，間違っているものには×を( )に記入しなさい。

(　) 1. レクリエーションの意味は，文字どおり「再び，創造すること」である。

(　) 2. レクリエーション活動は，クライアントの心身を活動的に機敏にさせる。

(　) 3. レクリエーションは，個人ではなく集団を対象にして計画されなければならない。

(　) 4. 危険を伴う活動には，ケアワーカーが付き添わねばならない。

(　) 5. レクリエーション活動後，クライアントの反応を聞くことは必ずしも重要ではない。

Dialogue　A Birthday Party for Mrs. Suzuki

Careworker:　Today is Mrs. Suzuki's birthday. She's 80. Let's all join together and sing "Happy Birthday" to her.

Everyone:　Happy birthday to you, happy birthday to you. Happy birthday Mrs. Suzuki, happy birthday to you.

Mrs. Suzuki:　Thank you all for this wonderful party. What a surprise! This room looks beautiful. Who did the decorations?

Careworker:　All your friends here did. Didn't they do a wonderful job? You should have seen how hard they worked at it.

Mrs. Suzuki:　Well, I can't tell you how happy you've all made me.

Careworker:　Okay, it's time for cake and ice cream. Take your seats everyone. I'll light the candles, one for each decade of your long life, Mrs. Suzuki. Now make a wish and blow out the candles.

Mr. Ando:　What did you wish for, Mrs. Suzuki?

Mrs. Suzuki:　I'm not supposed to tell you that, not if I want my wish to come true. But I'll tell you anyway. What I want most is many more years of health and happiness with all of my friends here.

Mrs. Kurata:　Why don't you open your presents now?

Mrs. Suzuki:　What? You have presents for me, too?

Mr. Ando:　We sure do. And we made them all ourselves with paper, scissors, felt-tip pens, glue and staples. Here, open mine first.

Mrs. Suzuki:　Well, look at that. A flowered hat made out of paper. It's really lovely. Let me try it on. How does it look?

Everyone:　It's beautiful.

覚えてほしい会話表現

* Congratulations on your birthday!　誕生日おめでとうございます。
* Please take your seats.　どうぞ着席してください。
* Okay, blow out the candles.　ろうそくの火を消してください。

知っておきたい英語

* recreation: re(反復)+ ラテン語の creo(=create)
  レクリエーションは「生活を明るく、楽しく、快適に送るため、すべての生活上の行い、活動」を言う。その意味で、単なる娯楽的な行為を越えて生きがいにつながる、種々の試みがなされる。日本においては、「社会福祉士及び介護福祉士法」(1987年)の制定に伴い、介護育成カリキュラムの中に、「レクリエーション指導法」が制定された。福祉現場でのレクリエーションの推進が重要視されている。

* keep an(one's) eye on:
  〜目を離さないでいる。eye は単数形であることに注意。

Practice

文房具・事務用品の英語を覚えよう。

シャープペンシル: (米) mechanical pencil, (英) propelling pencil.
ボールペン: ball-point pen
サインペン: felt-tipped pen (felt-tip)
蛍光ペン: highlighter, marking pen
ホチキス: stapler　日本語は発案者の名前である Benjamin B. Hotchkiss に因む商標名
セロテープ: cellulose[adhesive] tape，ただし(米)Scotch tape(商標名)，(英)Sellotape(商標名)
　　　　　　が普通名詞のように用いられる。
カッターナイフ: retractable knife　日本語は, cutter(裁断機, 器具の刃)＋knife(小刀, 短刀, 機械・
　　　　　　器具の刃) なので, いわゆる「馬から落ちて, 落馬して」と類語反復 tautology).
はさみ: scissors　複数形で用いる. cf. shears は大ばさみ。
消しゴム: eraser, (英)rubber: アメリカではこの意味で用いない。
ものさし: ruler
のり: paste
修正液: white-out, white correction fluid, Liquid Paper(商標名)
メモ帳: a memo pad (ひと綴りの), memo paper(用紙)
レポート用紙: writing paper
ルーズリーフ: loose-leaf notebook
便箋: letter paper, writing pad, stationery
封筒: envelope
透明ファイル: transparent file holder

Column

カタカナ語と福祉用語

　日本語は，漢字とひらがなとカタカナで表現します。この３つの表記法のうち，漢字はもちろんお隣の中国から輸入したもので，ひらがなは，平安初期に漢字草体からくずした草 (そう)の仮名をさらにくずした形で，主に女性が用いたもの。そしてカタカナは，平安初期に伊→イ，久→クのように，漢字の一部を取って作られました。このカタカナは現在では，外来語や和製語，擬音語の表記に用いられています。なぜか, 文具用品にもカタカナが多いのは，この章の Practice にあるとおりです。

　最近，カタカナ語の頻用が社会問題になる中で，特に公共性の高い場で使われる「外来語」について，国立国語研究所「外来語委員会」で論議され始め(2004 年～)，言い換えが提案されています。その中には福祉用語も含まれています。例えば，アイデンティー(自己認識, 独自性)，ケア(介護, 手当て)，デイサービス(日帰り介護)，ネグレクト(育児放棄, 無視)，バリアフリー(障壁なし)，メンタルヘルス(心の健康)，モラトリアム(猶予)，ノーマライゼイション(等生化, 等しく生きる社会の実現)など。

　これまで，日本人は多くの思想，社会システム，物，文化，食物などを外国から輸入して，苦労して日本語に訳してきました。例えば，今では「社会福祉」など自明のように使われている「社会」という日本語ですが，これは明治時代，日本にはない概念であった society を福地桜痴(新聞記者・劇作家)が訳したものです。

　国際化に伴って，日本にはなかった概念や，物質や，文化などが激流のように入ってくる時代です。言い換えを考えている暇はないのかもしれませんが，少なくとも，英語をそのまま使ったらカッコいい，などとは思わないほうがよいでしょう。

Unit 9 Helping People to Communicate

🔘 18

Communication means much more than mere conversation. True communication involves mutual understanding. When you communicate with someone, you actually get him/her to move into action.

As a care worker, you constantly need to communicate with clients who are old, ill and/or disabled. You need to find out what their true needs and feelings are. Language is not the only means of communication. Maintaining good eye contact is also essential. A client's eyes and facial expressions can tell you what he/she is really thinking. And remember: when a client speaks, listen carefully. Being a good listener is a vital part of your job. And don't forget human contact. Patting clients on the shoulder or taking them by the hand can go a long way toward relieving their distress and putting them at ease.

Some clients may tend to withdraw from others, but they are just as eager for warmth and love as everyone else. If a client is reluctant to talk with his/her fellow residents, your support can be very helpful. You can help two people start a conversation by introducing a topic of mutual interest. Hobbies, today's news, sports, music, art, and books are all good topics. When a client communicates with a family member, you, the caregiver, will often have to act as a kind of interpreter. Perhaps they haven't seen each other for a long time and have forgotten how to communicate. You can start things off by telling the family member about the client's life in the home. This will relax everyone and make communication easier.

Notes

mutual understanding: 相互理解　　eye contact: 視線を合わせること
pat on the shoulder: 肩を軽く叩く　　take ～ by the hand: 手を取る　　distress: 悩み
withdraw: 引っこむ, 引きこもる　　eager for: 強く望む
interpreter: 通訳者, 説明者(アクセントに注意)　　relax: くつろぐ

EXERCISES

1. Vocabulary Check

英語に相当する日本語をそれぞれ a ～ j から選びなさい。

1. withdraw ( )   a. 相互の
2. pat ( )   b. 表情
3. residents ( )   c. 意思疎通
4. interpreter ( )   d. くつろぐ
5. relative ( )   e. 安心させる
6. mutual ( )   f. 軽くたたく
7. communication ( )   g. 居住者
8. relieve ( )   h. 通訳者
9. relax ( )   i. 親類
10. facial expression ( ) j. 引きこもる

2. Comprehension Check

コミュニケーションについて以下のうち, 正しいものには○, 間違っているものには×を( )に記入しなさい。

( ) 1. コミュニケーションは, 相互理解によって実際に心が動かされ, 行動が起きることを含む。

( ) 2. コミュニケーションの手段は言葉だけである。

( ) 3. 相手の話に耳を傾けることは, コミュニケーションにおいて大切なことである。

( ) 4. クライアントは時々引きこもるが, 本当は暖かさや愛を求めている。

( ) 5. クライアントとその家族の関係は私的であるので, 介入しない方がよい。

Dialogue A Daughter Visits Her Mother at a Home

Daughter: Hi, Mom. How are you? (She takes her mother's hand.) You look great. The color has come back to your cheeks.

Mrs. Endo: I feel a lot better. I'm in good hands here.

Careworker: You should see how hard your mother works at her rehabilitation. If you have time, would you like to come and watch her do her exercises today?
(Mrs. Mori)

Daughter: I'd love to.

Mrs. Mori: Why don't you two go for a walk around the grounds? I'll come back when it's time for your rehabilitation, Mrs. Endo.

Daughter: Thanks for taking such good care of my mother.

Mrs. Mori: Not at all. It's my pleasure. Your mom's a wonderful person. We all love her. (Mrs. Mori leaves.)

Mrs. Endo: Thanks for visiting me today. Is everyone all right?

Daughter: Great. Shizuo is taking his entrance exams next month. But I seem to be more nervous about it than he is.

Mrs. Endo: Every parent goes through that. Remember when you took the exam for International University? I couldn't sleep for a week before. I'm sure Shizuo will do just fine. He's a smart boy.

(A while later)

Mrs. Mori: How was your walk? Not too tired for your exercises, I hope.

Mrs. Endo: Not at all. Besides, I want to show off for my daughter.

Daughter: And I'll be right there cheering you on, Mom.

知っておきたい英語

* conversation と communication の違い

    conversation は，会話・対話・対談と訳されるが，お付き合いや交流の意味が強い。一方，communication は伝達・意思疎通と訳され，情報・考え・意思等が相手に伝わることが必要である。会話はその場限りで終わるが，communication は，自分の言いたいことを相手に伝え，相手がそれを理解し，その言葉によって動くことが望まれる。

Practice

感情をあらわす英語と日本語を覚えよう

1. 次の表情を表す英語を，絵を参考に日本語で言いましょう。

happy(　　　　)　　　hurt(　　　　)　　　envious(　　　　)

withdrawn(　　　　)　　　thoughtful(　　　　)　　　lonely(　　　　)

surprised(　　　　)　　　satisfied(　　　　)　　　cold(　　　　)

2. 次の英語の意味を(　)に書き，その中からいくつかを選んで○の中に絵で表現してみましょう。

1. anxious (　　　　)　　2. sad (　　　　)　　3. optimistic (　　　　)
4. shocked (　　　　)　　5. lovestruck (　　　　)　　6. blissful (　　　　)
7. suspicious (　　　　)　　8. confident (　　　　)　　9. relieved (　　　　)

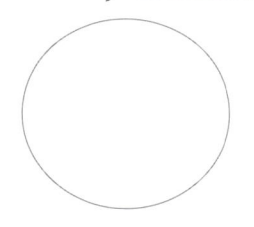

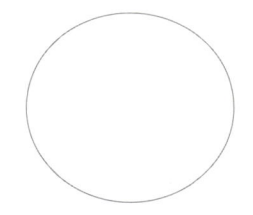

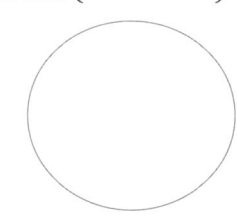

Column

body language: hand を使った表現

　手は人の体の部分で，最も表現豊かな力をもっています。また，手の一部である指は，文明の発達にも重要な役割を果たしてきました。もし，親指とその他の指とが向かいあうことがなかったとすれば，人間の社会はこれほどまでに発達しなかったでしょう。また，手は，この章の英文中にあるように body language として大切な機能を果たします。hand を含むいくつか動作表現をあげてみましょう。

　clap one's hand on one's forehead: 手で額をたたく＝「しまった」という気持ち。
　pat someone's hand: 相手の甲を軽くたたく＝「勇気」や「いたわり」を与える。ただし，主として上位者から下位者にする動作。
　take someone's hands in one's hands: 相手の両手を自分の手に包み込む＝「親しみ」「慰め」を表す。
　特に英語国民は，日本人に比べて動作表現が豊かなようです。でも，親しみを込めて相手の手を握って，"Get your hands off me!"(わたしの手を離してよ！)なんて言われないように。body language も相手次第です。

Unit 9　Helping People Communicate

Unit 10: Helping People Suffering from Disease and Illness

🔊 20

Careworkers play a vital role between clients and the doctors and nurses in charge of them. While undergoing treatment, a client is often entrusted to the care of a careworker. Many clients become frightened when faced with treatment, but your attention and care can go a long way towards reducing their anxiety and distress. You will often be called upon to get a client ready for a trip to a clinic or hospital outpatient department. It will be up to you to dress the patient and arrange for transportation and other necessities. You will also have to explain to the client what he/she can expect. In order to do this, you will need to clearly understand the nature of your client's illness. From the doctor or your supervisor, you must find out in advance what the diagnosis is, what treatment will be carried out, and where it will be given, and then pass this information on to your client.

A large part of your job as a caregiver is to assist your client's doctors and nurses. Such tasks as reporting changes in a client's condition, removing his/her mobility aids if any, undressing and dressing the client, changing his/her position, and helping the client get to and from the laboratory are all essential aspects of the treatment process. After the treatment, you must make sure you find out when the next treatment is scheduled for, what needs to be done for the client in the meantime, and so on.

Some people react to illness by becoming sad and depressed. Others become angry and aggressive. To prevent these emotional states, always speak in a confident, reassuring tone of voice and use gestures that soothe and comfort.

Notes

treatment: 治療　　entrust: (人)に…を任せる　　anxiety: 不安　　clinic: 個人・専門病院
hospital: 総合病院　　outpatient department: 外来　　transportation: (交通手段による)移動
diagnosis: 診断　　laboratory: 検査室, 実験室　　aggressive: 攻撃的な
emotional state: 情緒的な状態　　soothe: 落ち着かせる　　comfort: 慰める

EXERCISES

1. Vocabulary Check

英語に相当する日本語をそれぞれ a 〜 j から選びなさい。

1. gesture ( )
2. confident ( )
3. laboratory ( )
4. treatment ( )
5. diagnosis ( )
6. outpatient department ( )
7. distress ( )
8. agressive ( )
9. anxiety ( )
10. reassuring ( )

a. 苦痛
b. 攻撃的な
c. 安心させるような
d. 不安
e. 自信がある
f. 診断
g. 動作
h. 治療
i. 検査室
j. 外来

2. Comprehension Check

病気の人を介護する際の注意事項について以下のうち, 正しいものには○, 間違っているものには×を( )に記入しなさい。

( ) 1. 治療中のクライアントがもつ不安や苦痛を和らげるのはケアワーカーの役目である。

( ) 2. 病気にかかっているクライアントに対して, 通院に必要なことを準備するのはケアワーカーの仕事ではない。

( ) 3. ケアワーカーは, クライアントに付き添って病院へいくことは出来るが, 診察に際しては関与してはならない。

( ) 4. 治療予定や, 次の診断までにすることをクライアントにまかせてケアワーカーは確認しない。

( ) 5. クライアントを明るい気持ちにさせるために, しっかりと, 安心させる声で話しかけ, 慰め落ち着かせる動作をする。

Dialogue Helping a Client with a Toothache

Client (Mr. Sono): Mrs. Ueda, I have a throbbing toothache. I was up all night.
Mrs. Ueda: I'm sorry to hear that, Mr. Sono. I'll tell my supervisor and have her make a dentist's appointment.
Mr. Sono: I hate the dentist! Can't you just stop the pain?
Mrs. Ueda: You're going to have to have that bad tooth looked after sometime, Mr. Sono, so we might as well get it over with. I'm sure the dentist will take good care of you. They say he's excellent.
Mr. Sono: If you say so.
Mrs. Ueda: (Later) You're in luck, Mr. Sono. Since it's an emergency, the dentist will see you right away. I'll take you over there. Shall we get ready?

(At the dental clinic)

Dentist: Well, Mr. Sono, your wisdom tooth is pretty badly decayed. I think we'd better extract it.
Mr. Sono: Will it hurt?
Dentist: Hardly at all. Just a slight prick when I give you the local anesthetic. Okay, let's get started. Just relax and try to keep still. (Later) We're all finished, Mr. Sono. Now that wasn't so bad, was it? When the anesthetic wears off, you may feel a little pain. If it hurts too much, just take one of these painkillers. Come back in a few days and I'll take a look to make sure it's healing all right.
Mr. Sono: Thanks very much, doctor.

覚えて欲しい会話表現

> ＊症状を聞く表現
> How do you feel?　具合はどうですか？
> Where does it hurt?　どこが痛みますか？
> Can you describe the pain?　どんな痛みですか？
> Do you have any other symptoms?　ほかに症状はありませんか？
> Are you experiencing any dizziness?　めまいはしませんか？
> How is your balance?　ふらふらしますか？
> Any unsteadiness when you walk?　歩くのが不安定ですか？
> Do you have a temperature?　熱はありますか？

Practice

一般的な病気名と症状・医薬品などの英語表現を覚えよう
（身体の体系別疾患の英語は，Appendix 参照）

strained back(muscle): ぎっくり腰
strained finger: つき指
fracture: 骨折
burn: やけど
cognitive disorder: 認知症
cataract: 白内障
neuralgia: 神経痛
heart attack: 心臓発作
high(low) blood pressure: 高(低)血圧
sty: ものもらい
conjunctivitis: 結膜炎。(俗)pinkeye: はやり目。

bleeding: 出血
bruise: 打撲傷, 打ち身
gash: 長く深い傷
nick: 小さい切り傷
dizziness: めまい

bandage: 包帯
a Band-Aid(米: 商標), a sticking plaster(英): バンドエイド
gauze: ガーゼ
disinfectant: 消毒
injection: 注射

Column

病気の英語あれこれ

「病気」に相当する英語は，disease の他に，disorder, illness, sickness などがあります。これらの英語には少しずつニュアンスの違いがあります。illness と sickness は，病気である状態を表します。病名や伝染病で「....病」という場合には disease を，また，disorder は心やからだの不調や異常，障害を言います。精神の病は，通常 illness です。日本語でも「病気」は全身または一部が正常に機能を果たせなくなり，苦痛を訴える時に用います。「疾患」「疾病」も病気の意味ですが，「呼吸器疾患」「疾病保健」というように用います。

日本語の「病気」の「気」は，空気のように一定の形や体積を持っていない状態で，しかも特別の働きをするもの，という意味です。「病気」とは，気が病んでいる状態で，いつもは空気のようにあっても気がつかない状態が，病気になって始めて認識されるということでしょう。

英語の disease, disorder の dis- に注目してみましょう。これは，語の頭に位置する接頭辞と呼ばれるもので，その後に続く語に「欠如」の意味を持たせます。disease は ease(安楽)が dis-(欠如)した状態，disorder は order(からだの秩序)が dis- (欠如)した状態，を意味するのです。

医学の分野で用いる身体の構造・機能・病名は，ほとんどが，接頭辞＋(語根＝ことばの最小単位)から作られた連結形＋接尾辞で構成されています。巻末に付した病名を分析してみましょう。

Unit 11 Helping Children to Develop

Today, there are many different types of facility devoted to child care and development. These include day care centers, child welfare facilities, and centers for physically and mentally disabled children. In the past, children often entered these facilities for economic reasons, or, in the case of disabled children, because the parents could not adequately take care of the children at home.

Nowadays, the reasons children enter such facilities are much more varied. Single parents may not be able to afford to raise their children on their own. Family troubles can arrest a child's normal growth, making it preferable for the child to be raised in a more wholesome environment. Parents in two-income families where there are no grandparents to help with child rearing often rely on nursery schools or day care centers. Some parents enroll their children in day care simply because such facilities offer children more space to play in and more toys and friends to play with.

Whatever type of facility it is, and no matter what the reason behind the children's being there, trained child care workers must be on hand to ensure that our children get the best care possible.

Child abuse, including sexual abuse and neglect, is perhaps the most unsettling of the reasons for a child being entrusted to outside-the-home care these days. While such children are in your care, you may not be able to solve their complicated emotional problems, but you can help relieve some of their pain and distress and give them the warmth and love they so desperately need.

Notes

day care center: 通所施設(保育園, 保育所など)　　child welfare facility: 児童養護施設
center for physically and mentally disabled children: 肢体不自由児・知的障害児施設
afford: 余裕がある　　arrest: 止める　　two-income family: 共働き
enroll … in day care: …を保育園に入園させる
trained child care worker: (児童の養護・養育のための)訓練を受けた児童ケアワーカー
be on hand: (手助けのために)近くにいる　　child abuse: 児童虐待　　neglect: 放棄, ネグレクト

EXERCISES

1. Vocabulary Check

英語に相当する日本語を a 〜 j から選びなさい。

1. development (　)
2. emotional problem (　)
3. child abuse (　)
4. neglect (　)
5. child rearing (　)
6. economic reason (　)
7. nursery school (　)
8. child welfare facility (　)
9. wholesome environment (　)
10. raise (　)

a. 保育所
b. 情緒的問題
c. 経済的理由
d. 健全な環境
e. 放棄
f. 児童養護施設
g. 育てる
h. 発達
i. 子育て
j. 児童虐待

2. Comprehension Check

施設に入所する児童について以下のうち, 正しいものには○, 間違っているものには×を(　)に記入しなさい。

(　) 1. 過去において, 経済的理由で福祉施設に入所する児童はまれであった。

(　) 2. 現在, 親が子どもを保育所に入所させる理由のひとつに, 家庭では得られない教育・養育環境を与えたいということがある。

(　) 3. 児童が施設に入所する理由によって, 児童専門家の対処のし方が異なる。

(　) 4. 児童ケアワーカーは子どもたちの情緒的問題を解決しなければならない。

(　) 5. 児童はどのような状態であっても, 温かさや愛を強く求めている。

23
Dialogue   At a Nursery School

Child Care Specialist: What's the matter, Taka? Why aren't you playing with the other children?

Taka: I don't want to.

Specialist: But why not? Aren't you lonely over here all by yourself?

Taka: At least no one makes fun of me here.

Specialist: What do you mean? Who makes fun of you?

Taka: They all do. They tease me all the time. I hate them.

Specialist: I'm sure you don't hate them. You're just upset. What do they tease you about? Is it your leg braces?

Taka: Yes. They call me "cripple" all the time, and run circles around me, and point at my legs and laugh at me. I really do hate them.

Specialist: Well, that certainly isn't nice of them, is it? What would you like me to do about it?

Taka: Can't you just make them leave me alone? I just want to stay here by myself and play with the trains. I don't need those other kids.

Specialist: All right, I'll talk to them and tell them to stop teasing you. But isn't there anyone you'd like to play with?

Taka: Yuko's nice. She never teases me. But she's a girl. I'm sure she doesn't want to play trains with me.

Specialist: Well, you never know. I'll ask her. Or maybe you can do something else together. How about drawing and coloring? Or making things out of glue and paper? Wouldn't that be fun?

注）cripple は差別語であるが、ここでは保母がタブーの言葉であることを教えるために用いている。

知っておきたい英語

* abuse と neglect（虐待と放棄）

　かつて施設では、貧困と障害者の治療が入所の主な理由でしたが、最近、保育所を含めて、乳幼児虐待と育児放棄が最も重要な問題となっています。虐待は、性的虐待を含めて、西洋社会でも古くからありました。子供は父親の単なる財産としてみなされ、残酷で厳しい扱いを受け、幼少時から働き、責任を果たすことを求められ、体罰も当然とされていました。しかし、裕福な家庭や愛情のある家庭では、そのようなことに対しても同情心と庇護が必ず伴っていました。20世紀、特に、第2次世界大戦における残虐行為の反省から人権意識が高まりましたが、同時に、児童の人権も守ろうとする気運が高まり、わが国でも「児童憲章」が制定され(1951年)、国際連合でも「子どもの権利条約」が制定されました(1989年)。にもかかわらず、最近児童虐待・放棄の件数は増加する一方であり、その要因は複雑化する人間社会の病理を現しているかのようです。

Practice

'子どもの遊び' の英語を覚えよう
(英語に類似の遊びで言い換えられるもの, 日本独特のもの, 外来語であるもの等など)

じゃんけん: the game of " rock, paper, scissors" (英: "paper, stone, scissors")
かくれんぼ: hide-and-seek
おにごっこ: tag
お手玉: bean bags (tossing bean bags)
綾取り: cat's cradle
にらめっこ: staring contest
指相撲: thumb wrestling
押しくらまんじゅう: push-and-shove
まりつき: ball bouncing
双六: sugoroku (インドから中国を経て奈良時代に日本に伝わった)
カルタ: karuta (ポルトガル語 carta から)
メンコ: menko
福笑い: fukuwarai
羽根突き: battledore and shuttlecock (shuttlecock は羽根・バドミントンのシャトル)
こま回し: spin a top (spinning a top)
けんけん: hopping
鉄棒: chin-up bar (doing chin-bar)
ブランコ: swing (playing on the swing)
砂場: sandbox (playing on the sandbox)
縄跳び: jump roping, skip roping (doing jump roping)
ジャングルジム: jungle jim, monkey bars, 英: climbing frame (playing on the jungle jim)
すべり台: slide (playing on the slide)
　注: 特に記載していなければ, 動詞は play を使う。

Column

kindergarten はなぜ kindergarden ではないのか？

英語のつづりで間違いやすいのが kindergarten です。この語のもとはドイツ語の der Kindergarten です。それは das Kind (子どもの意味) の複数形である die Kinder と der Garten (庭の意味) の複合語です。むかしむかし, ゲルマン民族の大移動と共にヨーロッパ大陸を南下してきた人々の一部が, 現在のイギリスに住みつきました。ですから英語は元ドイツ語と言っても過言ではありません。庭を意味する Garten は英語では garden に変化したのですが, なぜか kindergarten のつづりはそのまま使われ続けました。いずれにせよ, 子どもは庭で遊ぶのが当然, ということなのでしょう。

日本語も「庭」の意味を汲んで, 「幼稚園」と訳されています。ドイツ語も英語も日本語も, 子どもの発達にとってもっとも大切なものは遊びであること, それも大気の中で, 体をのびのびと伸ばすことの出来る場所での遊びであることを言い表しています。

Unit 12
Helping with Domestic Duties in a Client's Home

🔘 24

As a careworker, you will often find yourself called to a client's home. On such assignments you will be asked to carry out such domestic duties as cooking, washing, cleaning, giving baths, receiving callers, shopping and even taking care of money and valuables. All of these are vital in keeping your client mentally and physically fit.

When working in a client's home, try to leave as many chores and tasks to your client as he/she can handle. A client may have trouble doing some of these tasks, and take a long time accomplishing them; but be patient. Although many of these daily duties may seem insignificant, your client will be prouder, happier, and more light-hearted if he/she can carry them out without help. Nothing contributes to a client's emotional stability better than doing things independently. Of course, with disabled or older clients, you will need to provide more active assistance.

Safety, both yours and your client's, should always be kept uppermost in your mind. Every home is filled with potential dangers. Furniture, doors, irons, electrical outlets, gas and electric stoves are all accidents waiting to happen. Neatness and cleanliness are also safety factors that can help prevent mishaps. If and when an accident or health emergency does occur, keep your head. Coolly analyze the situation to determine what happened and what needs to be done. Call for help and move your client to a safe place. If you are not qualified in first aid, don't attempt anything you're not sure about. You could cause your client further harm.

As for a client's money and valuables, it is best not to take charge of these on your own. If you think such items aren't secure enough, you can make a list and suggest a safer location.

Notes

domestic duty: 家事　　assignment: (割り当てられた)仕事　　valuables: 貴重品
chores: (複数形で)日常の家事(洗濯・掃除など)　　fit: 適合する ここでは「健康な」の意味。
insignificant: 無意味な　　mishap: 不運な事故　　analyze: 分析する　　first aid: 応急手当

EXERCISES

1. Vocabulary Check

英語に相当する日本語をそれぞれ a ～ j から選びなさい。

1. independence (　)
2. domestic duty (　)
3. safety (　)
4. first aid (　)
5. emergency (　)
6. mishap (　)
7. potential danger (　)
8. valuables (　)
9. insignificant (　)
10. qualified (　)

a. 無意味な
b. 家事
c. 隠れた危険
d. 貴重品
e. 有資格の
f. 緊急
g. 不運
h. 安全
i. 自立
j. 応急手当

2. Comprehension Check

家事援助について以下のうち，正しいものには○，間違っているものには×を(　)に記入しなさい。

(　) 1. 家事援助は，クライアントの心身の健康を維持するために重要である。

(　) 2. 毎日の家事はどんなことでも，クライアントに任さず，ケアワーカーが責任もってするのが望ましい。

(　) 3. 家庭ではいたるところに危険な事態を引き起こすことがあるので，安全がまず優先されなければならない。

(　) 4. 家庭で事故が起きた場合，ケアワーカーはまずクライアントに救急処置を施す必要がある。

(　) 5. お金や貴重品を預かってほしいとクライアントに頼まれた時は，責任もって預かる。

Unit 12　Helping with Domestic Duties in a Client's Home

Dialogue Helping a Client with Domestic Duties

Careworker: Hello, Mrs. Yamamoto. I'm Ms. Abe. I'm here to help you clean
(Ms. Abe) your house, do the washing or anything else you might need done.
Mrs. Yamamoto: Please, come in. The agency said they were sending somebody over today.
Ms. Abe: What a lovely home you have. Do you live all alone?
Mrs. Yamamoto: Yes. Unfortunately my husband passed away a few years ago.
Ms. Abe: From the looks of it, you don't need much help with cleaning. Your house is spotless. Did you do it all yourself?
Mrs. Yamamoto: I try to do as much as I can. But my best friend comes over pretty often to help me. She was here yesterday, in fact. She did the laundry, too.
Ms. Abe: Well, is there anything you'd like me to do for you today? Cook something, maybe, or do some shopping?
Mrs. Yamamoto: My friend took care of that for me, too. But if you could help me with my bath, I would be very grateful. It was so hot and muggy last night, I'd really like to take a nice hot bath.
Ms. Abe: I'd be happy to help. I'll just go and get the water ready.
Mrs. Yamamoto: (After the bath) Thanks for your help. I can manage most things myself, but I had hip surgery not too long ago, and I'm afraid I might slip and fall in the bath. By the way, would you like some tea and cake? My friend baked it herself.
Ms. Abe: Your friend really is a best friend, isn't she?

知っておきたい英語

＊専門領域で用いる省略語

私たちの周辺には省略語があふれています。例えば、英検(英語検定試験)、パソコン(personal computer)、セクハラ(sexual harassment)、DVD(digital versatile disc)，…言えば限りなくあります。福祉・介護・医療の領域でもよく見聞きする省略語のいくつかをあげてみます。そのフルスペリングを覚えることで英語に強くなるかもしれません。

QOL ＝ quality of life (生活の質)
ADL ＝ activities of daily living (日常生活動作)
SW ＝ social worker (ソーシャルワーカー)
PSW ＝ psychiatric social worker (精神医学ソーシャルワーカー)
MSW ＝ medical social worker(医療ソーシャルワーカー)
WHO ＝ the World Health Organization (世界保健機関)
DV ＝ domestic violence (家庭内暴力)
ADHD ＝ attention-deficit hyperactivity disorder (多動性障害)
LD ＝ learning disabilities (学習障害)

IQ ＝ intelligence quotient (知能指数)
EQ ＝ emotional quotient (こころの知能指数)
SARS ＝ severe acute respiratory syndrome (重症急性呼吸器症候群)
BSE ＝ bovine spongiform encephalopathy (狂牛病)
MRI ＝ magnetic resonance imaging (磁気共鳴断層撮影法)
HA ＝ hepatitis A (A型肝炎)
AIDS ＝ acquired immune deficiency syndrome(後天性免疫不全症候群)
etc, etc.=et cetera (= ラテン語)＝ and so forth ＝等等

注意：通常，省略語は普通名詞でも大文字で表します。

Practice
家事の英語を覚えよう。

＊掃除の表現
vacuum cleaner: 掃除機　　clean: 掃除する　　mop: モップをかける　　sweep: はく
wipe: 拭く　　dust: ほこりを取る　　scrub: ごしごしこする　　wastebasket: ごみ籠
garbage can: ごみ箱

＊洗濯と乾燥
washing machine: 洗濯機　　dryer: 乾燥機　　outdoor dryer: 物干し
clothespin(米), clothespeg(英): 洗濯ピン　　washing: 洗濯物　　hang out washing: 洗濯物を干す
iron: アイロン　　iron board: アイロン台

＊料理の用語は Unit 3 参照。

Column

welfare と farewell

welfare という英語の fare とは，人が暮らす，やっていく，という意味です。例えば，"How did you fare in the examination?"(試験はうまくいきましたか？)と言います。wel は well (うまく)という意味なので，welfare は，うまくやっていく，あるいはうまく暮らしていく，ということです。日本語の福祉は，福も祉も「しあわせ・さいわい」という意味です。ですから，社会福祉 (social welfare) とは，生活に困窮している人々，さまざまな障害のために生活をうまく送ることの出来ない人々に支援，育成，更正を社会的に行うことを意味します。そのために，国や地方自治体は法律を定め，資格認定された福祉の専門家によって，人々が wel (うまく) fare (暮らす) ように組織的に生活支援活動を行っているのです。

この welfare の wel と fare を逆にすると，farewell という別れの言葉になります。"Farewell"は "Good-bye" よりも古風な言い方で，長い別れの時に用いられる挨拶の言葉です。fare は元は「行く」という意味であり，farewell は well(よい) fare(旅をしてください)ということなのです。

welfare も farewell も福祉も，人々の生活が安全で幸せであるように，と祈る気持ちの込められた言葉です。

それでは, Farewell!

Appendix

移動補助器具 (mobility aids)

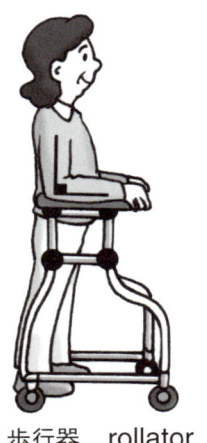

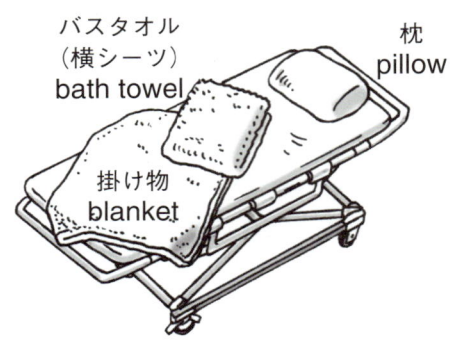

歩行器　rollator

バスタオル（横シーツ）bath towel
枕　pillow
掛け物　blanket
ストレッチャー　stretcher

トランスファーボード　transfer board

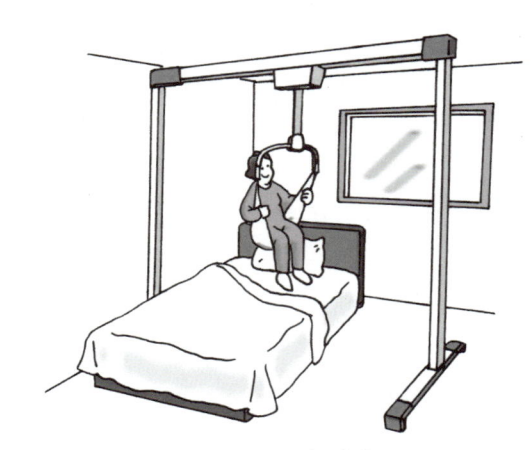

ホイスト　hoist

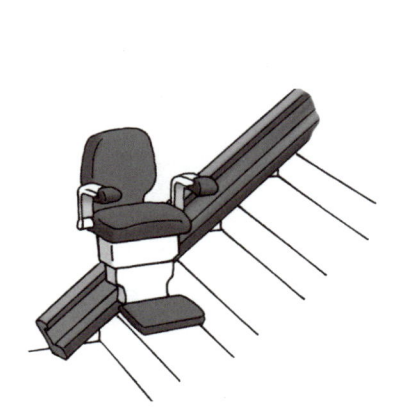

昇降器　stair-lift

スリング（吊り具）　sling

体位 (position)

臥位

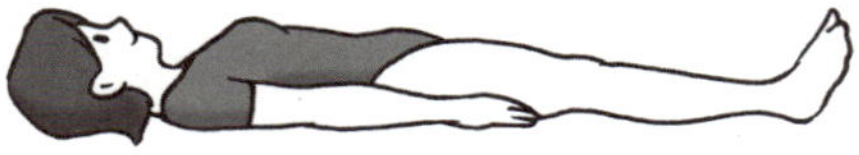

仰臥位　supination p., dorsal p. supine p.

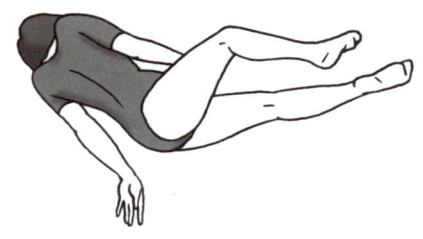

半腹臥位（シムズ位）
semiprone p. (Sims p.)

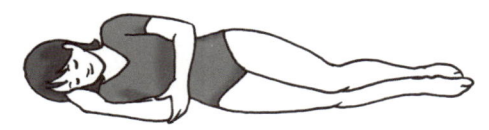

側腹臥位（横腹臥位）
side p./unilateral p./side lying p.

半背臥位（横腹臥位）　semisupine p.

腹臥位（伏臥位）　prone p.

立位

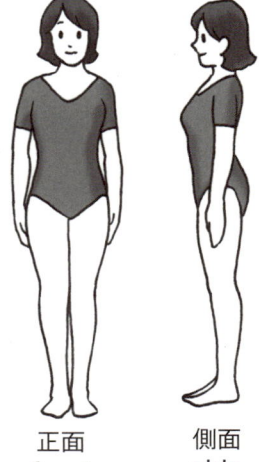

正面
front

側面
side

座位

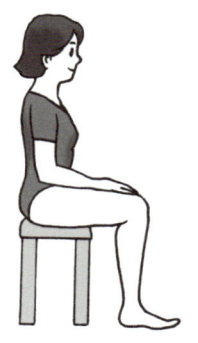

椅子座位
sitting p.

正座
sitting p. on the floor in Japanese fashion

長座位
long sitting p.

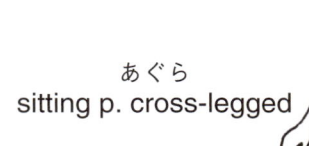

あぐら
sitting p. cross-legged

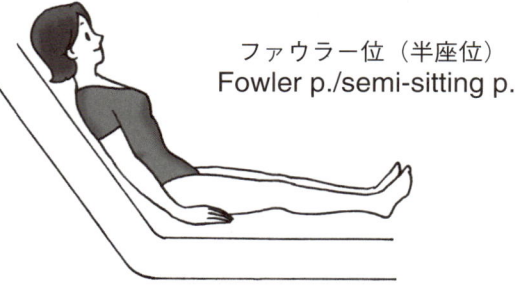

ファウラー位（半座位）
Fowler p./semi-sitting p.

Appendix 55

身体の解剖学的平面 (anatomical plane)

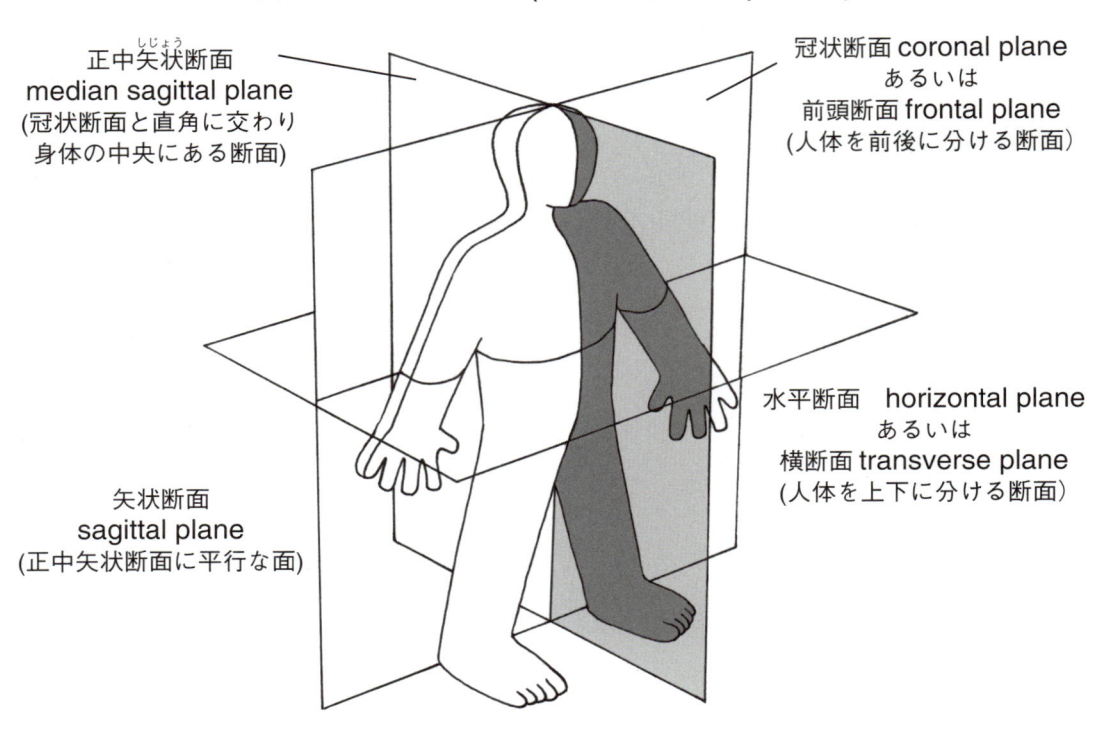

- 正中矢状断面 median sagittal plane
  (冠状断面と直角に交わり身体の中央にある断面)
- 冠状断面 coronal plane あるいは 前頭断面 frontal plane
  (人体を前後に分ける断面)
- 矢状断面 sagittal plane
  (正中矢状断面に平行な面)
- 水平断面 horizontal plane あるいは 横断面 transverse plane
  (人体を上下に分ける断面)

身体の方位 (anatomical direction)

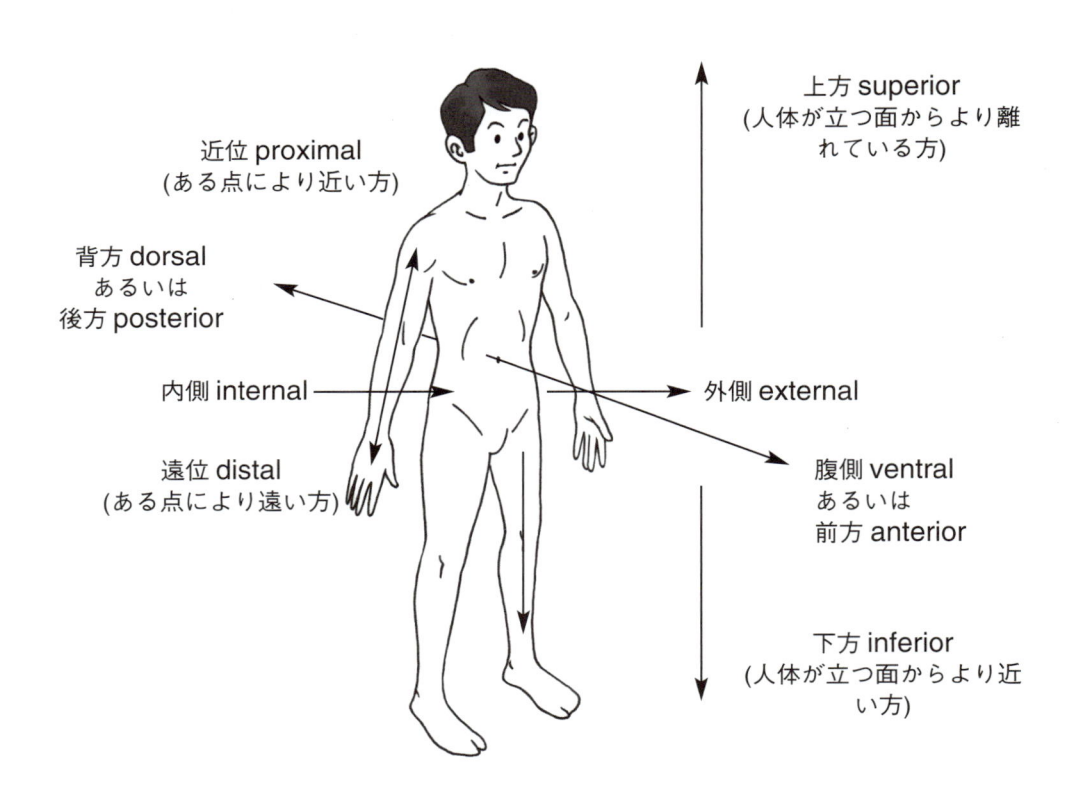

- 近位 proximal (ある点により近い方)
- 背方 dorsal あるいは 後方 posterior
- 内側 internal
- 遠位 distal (ある点により遠い方)
- 上方 superior (人体が立つ面からより離れている方)
- 外側 external
- 腹側 ventral あるいは 前方 anterior
- 下方 inferior (人体が立つ面からより近い方)

主要関節と部位 (main joints and regions of the body)

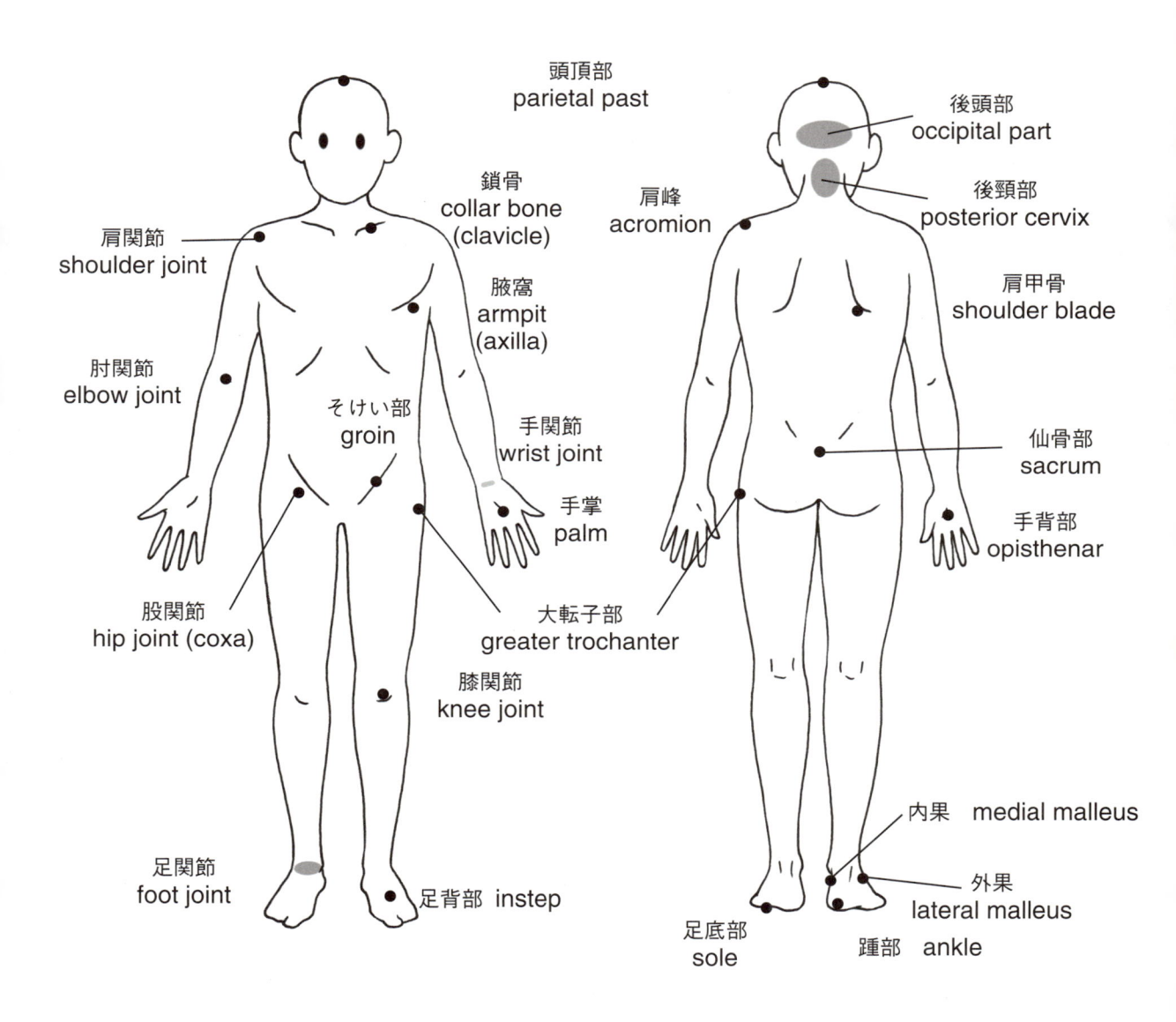

頭頂部	parietal past
鎖骨	collar bone (clavicle)
腋窩	armpit (axilla)
肩関節	shoulder joint
肘関節	elbow joint
そけい部	groin
手関節	wrist joint
手掌	palm
股関節	hip joint (coxa)
大転子部	greater trochanter
膝関節	knee joint
足関節	foot joint
足背部	instep
後頭部	occipital part
肩峰	acromion
後頸部	posterior cervix
肩甲骨	shoulder blade
仙骨部	sacrum
手背部	opisthenar
内果	medial malleus
外果	lateral malleus
足底部	sole
踵部	ankle

Appendix 57

運動の方向を示すことば (the direction of the body movement)

ヒトの関節は，曲げる，伸ばす，ねじるなどいろいろな動作をするが，基本的には3次元空間の3つの軸に関してそれぞれ2つずつ，合計6方向の運動を行う。人の関節の動作を次のように呼ぶ。

  外転 (abduction): 体幹から遠ざかる運動
  内転 (adduction): 体幹に近づく運動
  伸展 (extension): 伸ばす運動
  屈曲 (flexion): 曲げる運動
  内旋 (internal rotation): 四肢の長軸を中心にして内方への回転
  外旋 (external rotation): 四肢の長軸を中心にして外側への回転
  回内 (pronation): 手掌を下に向ける
  回外 (supination): 手掌を上に向ける
  内がえし (inversion): 足底を内側に向ける
  外がえし (eversion): 足底を外側に向ける

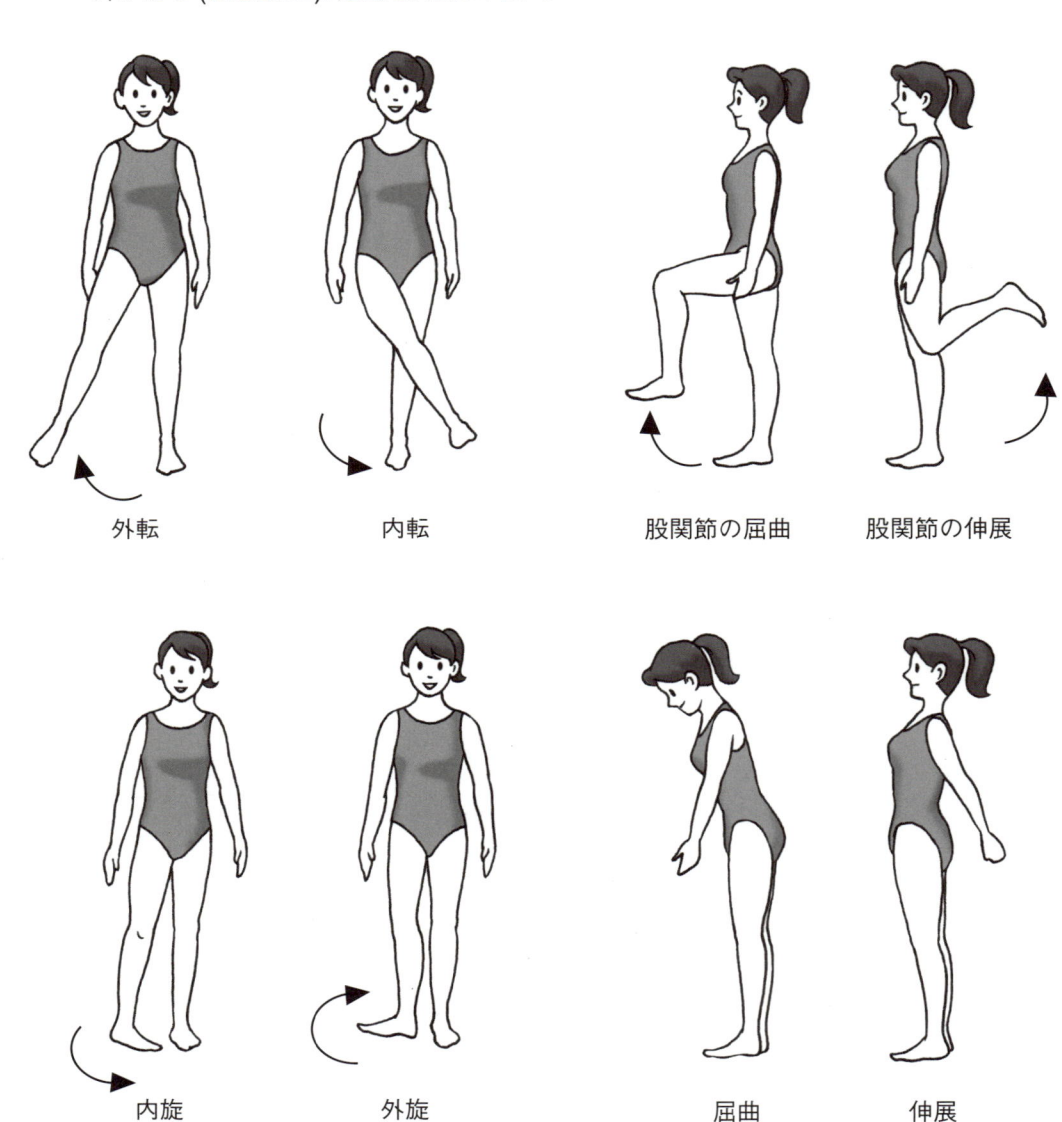

| 外転 | 内転 | 股関節の屈曲 | 股関節の伸展 |

| 内旋 | 外旋 | 屈曲 | 伸展 |

関節の構造と動き (the structure and movements of the joints)

関節のしくみ

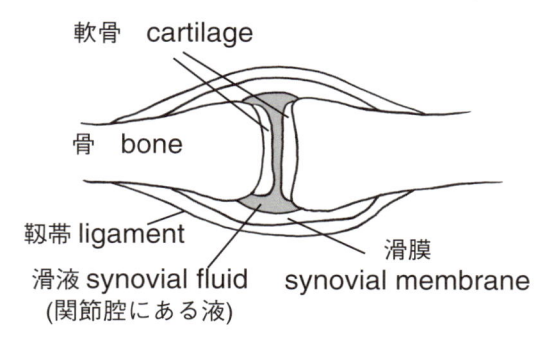

軟骨 cartilage
骨 bone
靱帯 ligament
滑液 synovial fluid (関節腔にある液)
滑膜 synovial membrane

骨と骨をつなぎ，運動をスムーズに行う重要な役割を果たしているのが関節 (joint) である。
ほとんどの関節には隙間があり，骨がうごきやすいようになっている。ある一定の可動域を設けることで運動の方向や範囲に制限を加え，筋肉や他の組織の損傷を防いでいる。

関節の構造と動きは，からだの各部でさまざまである。関節の構造により，動きは違ってくる。肩と肘，股，膝などの関節は曲げ (bent)，ねじり (twist)のほかに，内転 (adduction)，外転 (abduction)，回旋 (rotation)などの動きが可能である。

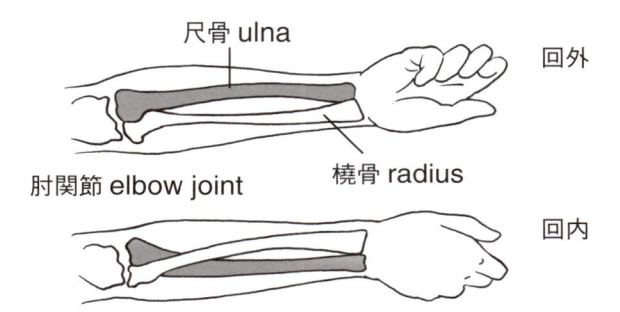

尺骨 ulna
肘関節 elbow joint
橈骨 radius
回外
回内

関節の種類

車軸関節 pivot joint

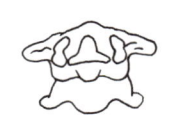

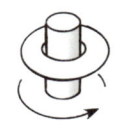

蝶番関節 hinge joint

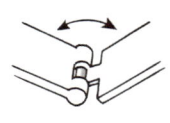

球窩関節 ball-and-socket joint

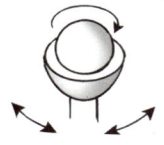

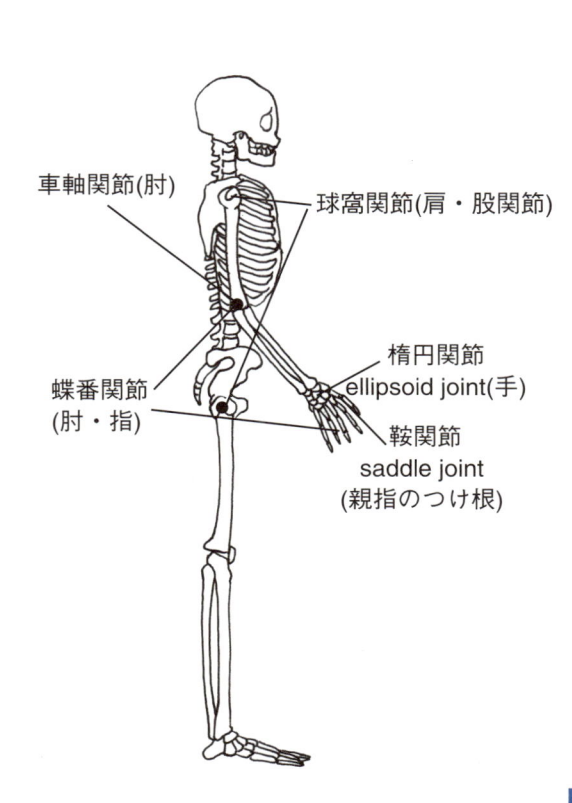

車軸関節(肘)
球窩関節(肩・股関節)
蝶番関節(肘・指)
楕円関節 ellipsoid joint(手)
鞍関節 saddle joint (親指のつけ根)

Appendix 59

病気の名称 (Disease)

●一般的な病気・症状
　下痢: diarrhea
　貧血: anemia
　便秘: constipation
　水虫: athlete's foot
　食中毒: food poisoning
　インフルエンザ: influenza(the flu)
　風邪: a cold

●こどもの病気
　風疹: rubella/German measles
　水疱瘡: chicken pox/varicella
　はしか: measles
　耳下腺炎(おたふくかぜ): mumps
　成長痛: growing pain
　自閉症: autism
　夜尿症: enuresis/(口)bed-wetting

●高齢者の病気
　老年性認知症: senile cognitive disorder
　老視(老眼): presbyopia
　老年性白内障: senile cataract
　老年性難聴: senile hearing loss
　関節炎: arthritis
　骨粗しょう症: osteoporosis
　腰痛: backache

●女性・男性・泌尿器の病気
　子宮筋腫: uterine myoma/fibroid of uterus
　前立腺肥大: prostatomegaly
　腎盂腎炎: pyelonephritis
　膀胱炎: cystitis

●骨と関節の病気
　むちうち損傷: whiplash injury
　アキレス腱断裂: rupture of Achilles' tendon
　椎間板ヘルニア: herniated disk

●精神疾患・こころの病気
　神経症: neurosis
　統合失調症: loss of coordination disorder
　不眠症: insomnia
　不安障害: anxiety disorder
　心的外傷後ストレス障害: PTSD
　　post-traumatic stress disorder
　摂食障害: eating disorder
　アパシー: apathy

●免疫異常による病気
　膠原病: collagen disease
　慢性関節リウーマチ: rheumatoid arthritis
　花粉症: pollinosis

●心臓・血管の病気
　狭心症: angina pectoris
　心筋梗塞: cardiac infarction
　心不全: heart failure
　動脈硬化症: arteriosclerosis
　不整脈: arrhythmia
　高血圧: hypertension

●呼吸器の病気:
　気管支炎: bronchitis
　ぜんそく: asthma
　肺炎: pneumonitis
　肺がん: lung cancer

●消化器の病気
　胃潰瘍: gastric ulcer
　十二指腸潰瘍: duodenal ulcer
　胃下垂: gastroptosis
　胃炎: gastritis
　肝炎: hepatitis
　肝硬変: cirrhosis
　虫垂炎: vermifrom appendicitis

●脳・神経系の病気
　脳卒中: cerebral apolexy
　脳梗塞: cerebral infarction
　くも膜下出血: subarachnoid hemorrhage
　神経痛: neuralgia
　パーキンソン病: Parkinson's disease

●眼・耳・鼻・口腔の病気
　近視: myopia/nearsightedness
　遠視: hyperoptia/far-sightedness
　斜視: astigmatism
　白内障: cataract
　結膜炎: conjunctivitis/(口)pinkeye
　虫歯(う食症): decayed tooth
　歯周病(歯槽膿漏): pyorrhea
　中耳炎: otitis media
　鼻炎: rhinitis
　扁桃腺炎: tonsilitis

●皮膚の病気
　じんましん: hives
　湿疹: eczema
　アトピー性皮膚炎: atopic dermatitis

●ホルモン・代謝異常の病気
　甲状腺機能亢進症: hyperthyrodism
　肥満症: obesity
　脚気: beri beri

●性感染症(STD)
　エイズ(後天性免疫不全症候群): AIDS
　　(acquired immune deficiency syndrome)

専門医 (specialist)

神経科医: neurologist
脳神経外科: neurosurgeon
精神科医: psychiatrist
　（精神分析専門医は psychoanalyst/analyst）

呼吸器科専門医: respiratory disease specialist
心臓専門医: cardiologist
胃腸科専門医: gastroenterologist

内科医: internist
外科医: surgeon
整形外科医: orthopedic surgeon
形成外科医: plastic surgeon
美容整形外科医: cosmetic surgeon
麻酔科医: anesthesiologist
放射線科医: radiologist

小児科医: pediatrician
老人病専門医: geriatrician/geriatrist

内分泌専門医: endocrinologist
リューマチ専門医: rheumatologist
血液専門医: hematologist
アレルギー専門医: allergy specialist/allergist
腫瘍（がん）専門医: oncologist

眼科医: ophthalmologist*
　* 検眼士, 視力矯正士は optometrist/（英）ophthalmic optician で, 処方によってめがねを調整する人は optician である。いずれも M.D.（医師）ではない。

耳鼻咽喉科医: ear-nose-throat doctor/NET doctor/otorhinolaryngologist
口腔外科医: oral surgeon
歯科医: dentist
小児歯科医: children's dentist
矯正歯科医: orthodontist

皮膚科医: dermatologist

泌尿器科医: urologist
腎臓専門医: nephrologist
肛門科医: proctologist
産科医: obstetrician
婦人科医: gynecologist

脊柱指圧療法師: chiropractor
接骨医: osteopathist
臨床心理療法士: clinical psychologist
　　　M.D.ではないが Doctor と名乗ることがある。

Appendix 61

福祉関連の職種と施設
(the occupations and institutions related to social welfare)

＊児童福祉施設

child welfare institution(facility): 児童福祉施設
　児童福祉法7条による14種類の施設がある。家庭で児童を養護する責任を果たせない児童を，家庭に代わって養護，養育する。環境に問題がある児童，心身に障害がある児童，情緒・行動に問題のある児童，一般の児童を対象に分かれ，入所，通所形態をとっている。以下，いくつかを挙げる。

day nursery(米), day care center(米) day care nursery(英), nursery school(英):
　保育所，託児所(通称，保育園，保育者の委託を受けて，保育が不十分な乳児・幼児を保育する施設。)

children's home, nursing home: 養護施設(満1歳から満18際未満で，保護者のいない児童，虐待を受けている児童，好ましくない環境にいる児童を養護・養育する施設。現在では，家庭崩壊の結果，入所する児童が多い。)

baby's home: 乳児院(家庭で保育を受けられない乳児を入院させ，養育する施設。)

home for mentally disabled children: 知的障害児施設(知的障害のある児童を保護し，独立・自活できるよう知識・技能を与えることを目的とする。)

rehabilitation facility for children with emotional disabilities: 肢体不自由児施設(上・下肢，体幹の機能障害がある児童を治療する。医療法による病院としての機能をもち，併せて，独立，自活を目指し生活・職業指導を行う。)

facility for children with visual and hearing disabilities: 盲聾唖児童施設(視覚；強度の弱視を含む/聴覚；強度の難聴を含む，に障害をもつ児童を保護，指導・援助して独立・自活を目ざす。)

school for disabled children: 養護学校(知的障害児・肢体不自由児。病弱児(虚弱児を含む)の障害や特性に従って，適切な教育，機能訓練を行い，社会参加に向けた発達を目指す。)

＊児童に関わる専門職の呼称

child welfare officer: 児童ソーシャルワーカー(非行・不登校・ひきこもり・養育など児童と保護者が抱える問題を適切な調査・指導・問題解決に努める福祉専門のソーシャルワーカー。)

nursery teacher: 保育士(児童福祉施設において，児童の発達段階に合わせて指導，援助，自立を促す保育に従事する専門識者。)

child consultant: 児童相談員(保育士と共に，児童に関するさまざまの問題を，家庭，学校，児童本人から相談を受け，基本的な生活習慣を身につけさせ，学習指導を行う。)

school nurse: 養護教諭(知的障害児，肢体不自由児，病弱・身体虚弱児を教育指導する教員。)

＊福祉関連の専門職

social worker: ソーシャルワーカー(社会福祉施設,福祉事務所,公的機関等で,社会生活上の問題・困難を抱えている人の相談に応じ,助言や支援を行う。国家資格として1987年に社会福祉士＜名称独占＞が創設された。)

psychiatric social worker(PSW): 精神科ソーシャルワーカー(精神病院,保健所等で精神障害者とその家族が抱える問題を解決し,入院患者に対しては退院,社会復帰を支援する。かつては,医療ソーシャルワーカーの一部であったが,1997年に精神保健福祉士＜名称独占＞が創設され,PSWとして独立した。) cf.介護関連はUnit 2。

medical social worker(MSW): 医療ソーシャルワーカー(ソーシャルワーカーの内,医療機関で働く専門職。患者とその家族のもつ病気とその周辺のさまざまな問題に関して相談にのり,援助する。)

その他の職種
既出以外に,福祉関連の職種には, doctor(=medical doctor: 開業医はmedical practitioner), dentist(歯科医), nurse(看護士), physical therapist(=PT: 理学療法士), occupational therapist(=OT: 作業療法士), speech therapist(=ST:言語聴覚療法士), orthoptist(視能訓練士), music therapist(音楽療法士), sign-language interpreter(手話通訳士)等々,広範な福祉領域を反映して種々の仕事がある。
cf・介護関連はUnit 2, 栄養関連はUnit 3。

licensed nursing care worker: 介護福祉士: p.12「知っておきたい英語」参照。「社会福祉士および介護福祉士法(1987)による名称独占の資格。

home help(helper): ホームヘルパー（現在は, 高齢者, 身体障害者, 心身障害児, 難病患者等, 利用者の家庭を訪問し, 身体介護・家事・相談・援助を行う．介護技術の質向上を目指して1995年にホームヘルパー養成カリキュラムが改正された．

＊福祉関連の施設の呼称

fee-paying elderly people's home: 有料老人ホーム
home for the elder people's home: 老人ホーム
special nursing home for the elderly: 特別養護老人ホーム
facility of health care services for the elderly: 老人保健施設
day-care center for the elderly: 老人日帰り介護施設
day-care center: 高齢者・身体障害者の憩いの家
day-service center: デイサービス施設
home(facilities)for the care of the elderly: 高齢者介護施設
support center for home care[home care services support center]: 在宅支援センター
a low-expense home for the elderly: ケアハウス,介護利用型軽費老人ホーム
  cf. 老人の英語訳は, old people 以外に, the aged, the elderly, elderly people などがある。日本語でも人権や人格を反映して,老人と呼ばずに,高齢者や熟年層と呼ぶことと共通している。

> 著作権法上、無断複写・複製は禁じられています。

A Helping Hand — Comprehensive English for Caregivers [B-557]
福祉・介護系学生のための総合英語

1　刷	2007年1月24日	
15　刷	2024年9月6日	
著　者	清水雅子 Masako Shimizu	
発行者	南雲　一範　Kazunori Nagumo	
発行所	株式会社　南雲堂	
	〒162-0801　東京都新宿区山吹町361	
	NAN'UN-DO Publishing Co., Ltd.	
	361 Yamabuki-cho, Shinjuku-ku, Tokyo 162-0801, Japan	
	振替口座：00160-0-46863	
	TEL: 03-3268-2311（代表）／FAX: 03-3269-2486	
	編集者　TH	
印刷所	株式会社 教文堂	
製版所	Kraft	
装　丁	Nスタジオ	
イラスト	©PALMS	
検　印	省　略	
コード	ISBN978-4-523-17557-5　C0082	

E-mail　nanundo@post.email.ne.jp
URL　http://www.nanun-do.co.jp